Kids Supernaturally Natural
MENTORING CATERPILLARS INTO BUTTERFLIES

Virginia Humphreys
with Tammy Searle

All profits from the sale of this book are funding internships and discipleship training schools for families, youth, and children.

Kids Supernaturally Natural

Self-Published via Amazon's CreateSpace

©2015 All rights reserved

To order additional copies contact:

Tammy Searle
tammydsearle@gmail.com
(970) 903-8104
841 Hersh Ave
Pagosa Springs, CO
81147

1st Printing November 2015
2nd Printing November 2016

All rights reserved. This book is protected by the copyright laws of the United States of America. This book may not be copied or reprinted for commercial gain or profit. The use of short quotations or occasional page copying for personal or group study is permitted and encouraged.
Unless otherwise identified, Scripture quotations are from The Christian Growth Study Bible, New International Study Version ®, copyright © The Zondervan Corporation. The Holy Bible, New International Version ®, Copyright
© 1973, 1978, 1984 by the International Bible Society.

THE MESSAGE: The Bible in Contemporary Language Copyright © 2002 by Eugene H. Peterson, all rights reserved.
THE MESSAGE, Numbered edition copyright © 2005

Illustrated by Easton Humphreys and Brandon Pollard

Design and Layout by Nathanael Ward

To all my grandchildren

Tasha, David, Brandon, Colton, Cassie, Easton, Daniel, Mia, Mathias, Josiah, & Vanessa

My prayer is that you carry the Message through the next generation if the Lord does not come soon.

Dedication

I dedicate this book to the three men in my life who have stood by me and encouraged me for so many years.

First to my husband, my best friend of 47 years Dick Humphreys who allowed me the freedom to chase God, to learn His passions, to feel His presence and always encouraged me even in hard times. Even now as he is at home with Jesus, he encourages me because I have learned from him over the years.

To my very good friends and Pastors Alan DeBoer, Restoration Fellowship and Pastor Lenny LaGuardia, International House of Prayer who sometimes embraced a life of discomfort, to ultimately win the prize of seeing passionate sons and daughters of the Highest King. Thank you so much and in your words Lenny, "I love each of you, you are my heroes."

Acknowledgements

I especially want to acknowledge my son Jeremy and his wife Elea Humphreys, YWAM Whitsunday for their continued exhortation and encouragement; for giving me more passion and insight into the nations and God's heart for all people through missions.

To my good friends Jack and Tammy Searle, thanks for believing in me, hanging with me for so many years and giving me room to grow. Thank you for all your help in completing this project. I could not have done it without either of you or your family. I am blessed to call you my friends.

Staff and Elders at Restoration Fellowship and your willingness to pay the price and pave the way for fruit beyond belief; you guys have been such a blessing to many.

To Angie Ranson for your faithful service to our children.

It is with my deepest gratitude I say thanks to all of your intercessors who have prayed for this for so many years, no way could this have happened without your dedication to empowering children. You know who you are and how much you are loved.

Mark, Sharon and Amie for all the hours and hours of editing, your gift is so appreciated and so cherished.

I want to thank all four of my children. Daughters Diane and Deb and our two sons Jason and Jeremy, I love you all so much, you are a taste of heaven on earth for me.

Forward

Tracy and I have devoted much time and energy over many years in ministry to children. I believe Jesus is clearly releasing the children of this generation. He is unlocking their hearts and revealing their identity as passionate sons and daughters of our most High King. He is taking us to new heights of our understanding of ministry to children to be able to walk in deeper intimacy with our Bridegroom King.

Virginia's book, "Mentoring Caterpillars into Butterflies" is truly awesome! She captures and unveils the truths in ministry to children in a clear, easy-to-understand format while maintaining scriptural integrity. She helps you to understand how to create an atmosphere of grace where Jesus is the most natural response so that signs and wonders naturally follow.

The church is in need of a radical transformation of the way we minister to children. You will be overwhelmed at the authentic display of a genuine dependence on God. Whenever the presence of God enables a child to be free before Him, you cannot help but be amazed at what a wonderful Savior.

As a forerunner in children's ministry she will fan your passion as the eyes of your heart are enlightened to the simplicity of putting your trust in the Holy Spirit and allowing Him to minister to your children.

Pastor Lenny LaGuardia
Executive Director Children's Equipping Center
International House of Prayer, Kansas City, MO

After watching, observing and rejoicing with the children that have opened their hearts to receive the supernatural into their lives in a natural way, this book is highly recommended for anyone desiring to bring children deeper into the heart of God and intimacy with our Heavenly Father.

Virginia shares many personal experiences that will help your own faith level to rise and to bring the courage to step out in faith to whatever the Lord calls you.

Children are definitely "wet cement" and as we pour the truths of the Kingdom of God into their lives, it will "harden" a firm foundation for them that will stand the test of time, circumstances and battles. This book gives you practical steps and encouraging affirmation as you pursue the path God has you on in seeding into the next generation.

Pastors Al and Sharon DeBoer
Restoration Fellowship
Pagosa Springs, Colorado

This practical, thought-provoking book presents a new paradigm for children's ministry and offers practical steps for those serious about empowering their children.

Virginia has over 20 years' experience in mentoring children and answers many of the questions facing every children's ministry. She advocates the need to regard children as full participants in their faith while developing an intimate personal love relationship with their heavenly Father.

Using personal examples in most aspects of children's ministry, this book provides step by step guidance and creative application exercises to help churches develop not only a thriving children's ministry, but one that produces sons and daughters with hearts abandoned to God, hearing His voice and willing to "go" and serve.

This book is for those desiring to raise a generation longing for the presence of God. It will change the way you minister to children.

Jeremy and Elea Humphreys
Base Directors and International Speakers
Youth with a Mission Whitsunday
Airlie Beach, QLD, Australia

Introduction

I want to encourage you in this: the simple fact that you have this book in your hand and you're reading this now indicates that you probably have an interest in raising up the next generation. I don't know you, but I bet that you have a heart desire to minister to children. Maybe you already are involved in Sunday School classes, after school outreaches or Vacation Bible Schools. Good for you! I applaud you! If God asked me to assign seats in Heaven, I would put you in the front row!

Be encouraged, you are making a difference. You are part of the laborers that we pray the Lord into the harvest. The children in your sphere of influence are very capable of receiving the outpouring of the Father's love through encounters of His presence. They easily and readily recognize and hear His voice. Their pure hearts are sponges for soaking up the desires of His heart for an intimate relationship. Children naturally hunger for more when they are in an environment that encourages knowing who they are and who He is.

So what you hold in your hands is a guide that communicates the journey that my good friend Virginia Humphreys has been on while raising up the next generation to carry and operate in the things of God. I am privileged to have worked with her for a few years of this journey. I am honored that she asked me to share my heart and experiences in a couple chapters of this book.

Enjoy! Keep it simple and keep showing up!

Tammy Searle

A Word from the Author

A children's pastor came up to me at a conference where I was speaking and asked, "Would it be ok if I could get your contact information, we are so anxious for our children to move in the power of the Holy Spirit and we just don't know how to begin?" How I wish I could tell her how to begin! It wasn't anything we did! You cannot get it from a book but only from seeking the voice of your Father and trusting in the power of Holy Spirit to lead you, guide you and direct your steps. Listening to the voice of God and obeying.

I remember I had just taken over the position as Children's Ministry Director at my church. It is not about a title but about an anointing, a calling to minister to children. My son called from Central Asia where he was involved in youth work. He told me an about a conference he thought I should go to in Kansas City.

"It is all about a move of God among children." He said it was at the International House of Prayer, had I heard of it? In those days few had heard that this little place even existed in Kansas City but yes I had. In September of 1999, they had begun 24/7 prayer and worship there. Hmm… that was kind of wild in the United States of America! He said they had a new children's pastor and he was teaching children about prayer and how to follow the Holy Spirit. I had trained as a children's pastor with a large ministry years before and in my spirit I had always known children could go deeper with God. Having just recently finished a Crossroads Discipleship Training School with Youth with a Mission in Perth, Australia, I had seen this modeled.

We gathered the children together on Wednesday afternoons, we would pray and ask God for direction, for wisdom for His children, and then one of us would preach to the children. We loved to take a microphone, fifteen kids or so down to the train station, sing and dance, and then share the Word or testimony. A lot of people would stop and listen to the children share a testimony; some children would even preach. We saw people saved and healed, words of knowledge and children prophesying. God's greatest joy has to be to see a child's unwavering trust. I would never dream that this could be done in a church setting knowing that less than 10% of children attending any Sunday school will ever receive any more than that. The children we worked with were MK's (Missionary Kids) and we were preparing them for outreach. They needed to be able to accompany their parents going into India and Southeast Asia to be part of a ministry team and to preach the Gospel with power. They needed to know the key to moving in God's power, so that signs and wonders and miracles would follow them anywhere.

These kids were amazing, they loved God so much. We, as a team, constantly poured into them the truths of the scriptures, the same thing their parents were learning in their school. There were no three point lessons plans with an exciting conclusion. There was no curriculum, no puppets, and no gospel magic; just the truth in a kid's language, prayer, and intercession. Their parents were some of the most intense, radical, and passionate people you could meet.

I remember a day some of us had the opportunity to sail on a small yacht to a little island about three hours from Perth. After we had been at sea for a while, one of the young girls of around twelve had crawled out on a boom and was lying there, kind of like in the movie Titanic.

She called back and said to us, "O-ooh, how I wish we could see dolphins!"

I yelled back at her, "Don't wish, cry out to your Father in Heaven. He wants to bless you. He wants you to ask Him, not wish! Ask Him for the desire of your heart. God put those desires there."

The skipper then turned to me and said, "Not too likely, Miss, to see dolphin in this sort of water, not at all! I have been sailing these waters a good long time. Nope it won't happen!"

In a while he was astounded to shout out for us to "see the school of dolphin off the starboard bow."

Boy, did we rejoice and thank God for the miracle in answering a child's prayer. We went ahead with our day and enjoyed a nice picnic on a remote island. We caught a brisk wind in our sails which carried us back to Perth much faster than we had sailed over to the island. The skipper was skillfully maneuvering our big boat into the harbor when we saw a dolphin jumping, squealing, and doing all sorts of tricks. It was a one-man show! This little guy followed us all the way into the boat slip with his chattering and antics. He was so cute! We praised God for the double portion of blessing in answering the prayer of faith of one of His children. Oh, I know what you are thinking, "Well it just happened, coincidence." This seasoned skipper told us he had never seen anything like it in all the years he had made sail; occasionally dolphins in the sea, but never had he seen one in that harbor.

Another time we were all in a local park. There was a lady named Jules who could change a tire, or rebuild an engine on a truck, yet she was the kindest, most gentle person when it came to children. The kids loved her and so did we. She had taken all the kids to a park one morning while we had lectures. The children had made pancakes for our group in this park. All of a sudden, several of our children were walking around and looking at the grass. I asked what they were looking for and one of the children told me that Maggie had lost an emerald from her wedding ring. I suggested we all needed to pray so we could find that stone. As soon as we finished praying, I looked down and there was the biggest emerald I had ever seen.

A few days later we were at a lake and some children came running excitedly to me.

"Remember at the park the other day, Virginia, you told us to pray so we could find the emerald? Well, Lars lost his glasses in the muddy lake and we did what you said and there were his glasses".

They were jumping up and down. "We found them! We didn't even have to look; they were just there."

Signs, wonders and miracles occurred because of faith and trust in their Father. Oh, that we could become like little children! We could learn so much about faith.

Our Wednesday outreach consisted of many different things. One of our teams knocked on doors, offered to wash dishes, go get groceries, mow lawns, and always offered prayer. I remember they reported knocking on a door and this young guy told them he had been waiting for them. He had had an encounter with Jesus and had been healed three days earlier.

Pointing to his wheelchair, he explained to the MK's that Jesus told him in an audible voice, "that someone would come in three days and let him know what had happened."

I had been thinking about the conference in Kansas City that my son spoke of and I asked him, "When is it?" "It starts in two days," he said.

"Well," I thought, "that would have to be a miracle for sure. I have no money to attend and it would have to be approved for the church to pay for it."

Logistically there just was not time to arrange something like that.

I hung up the phone thinking, "There is no way, Lord, unless you show me your hand is in this and you indeed desire that I would go."

Then the phone rang!

My friend Jane asked me, "Virginia, I am going to Kansas City in the morning by myself. My husband was to go with me but he has been called out of town on business. I have to get my house ready to sell, and I was wondering if you could go along and keep me company? I really need someone to drive a car back for me, I cannot tow it. I will need to drive a U-Haul. I will pay for everything!"

I laughed and said, "Yes, sure if I can attend a conference on Friday, Saturday and Sunday."

It turns out that her home was very near the International House of Prayer so it was no bother at all. God is so good and sometimes quick to respond, just knowing we are willing. I did not have to ponder whether or not it was His will, I just went. I knew it was!

CONTENTS:

Chapter 1	God's Heart for Today	23
Chapter 2	Passion for Prayer and Intercession	30
Chapter 3	Clean Fresh Water	36
Chapter 4	Don't Stop Until the Kids Do!	41
Chapter 5	Engaging Feelings to Feel Better	47
Chapter 6	Who Said You Can't Dance?	51
Chapter 7	Passion for War	55
Chapter 8	Dude, Just Kick Satan in the Butt!	60
Chapter 9	The Only Book	63
Chapter 10	Meaningless Colors and Numbers	68
Chapter 11	Lessons in Art, Dreams & Visions	73
Chapter 12	Fasting - Encountering God's Love	77
Chapter 13	Caterpillars and Butterflies	81
Chapter 14	Fire on the Rock	88
Chapter 15	We Do What We Do and That's All That We Do	92
Chapter 16	Organizing a Sleep Out	98
Chapter 17	How to Chase After God's Heart	110
Chapter 18	A Strategic and Intentional Effort	119

Chapter 1
God's Heart for Today

THIS HAS ALWAYS BEEN GOD'S HEART

We were ministering at a camp in the mountains of Colorado a few years ago. It rained, no, it poured, for two days. The evening ministry session was intense as we pulled the sides of the tent down. It was warm and the thunder and lightning crashed all around us. There was so much rain there were worms coming up out of the dry ground in the tent. We ministered healing of the broken hearted among the children suffering from divorce, abandonment, and hurtful things in their lives they have no control over. Many children wept. Many on our team wept for and with the children. The next morning at breakfast the owner of the camp approached me and said that suddenly most of their horses were ill with fever and would we pray for them? A strange request, but sure, I said, I would put my intercessors on it. I do not ever minister without a team of intercessors; results are always better with a passionate covering!

That night, was again, an intense time of ministering healing and deliverance with the children and adults. I do need to pause here and let you know that deliverance with children is much different than some of you may be thinking, but I will cover that in more detail later on. The next morning the owner came again and asked for prayer for their horses, now even more were sick!

"You don't understand, we have 100 special needs kids coming next week and the ministry with them all revolves around horses." Now she got my attention! Suddenly the Lord gave me insight into the situation. When we had prayed deliverance for the children we had not given instructions to the enemy as to where he should relocate. At the evening meeting, I explained the situation to the children and the leaders. We typically play an icebreaker game but I asked the children to fast from games that evening and use the time for prayer. We prayed collectively as a group and the children were very bold in their prayers, we danced, we worshiped. We then broke up into smaller teams and did some heavy intercession. The next morning, I inquired about the horses, and was told they were all healed but six who still had fever. We prayed once again at the morning session, and by that evening there was not a sick horse at the camp. Children love it when they can go deep with God and be part of what He is doing. We so underestimate their love and understanding of the Father.

This generation has indeed been born for signs and wonders! Children are hungry for the supernatural, for the prophetic, because they are bombarded by it in the secular world and what a blessing for the church. The scriptures are coming to pass, *"That you will know without question that I am in the thick of life with Israel. That I am your God, yes your God, the one and only God. Never again will my people be despised."* (Joel 2:25–30, MSG). Children are hungry for God! Children are hungry to hear God! Children want to be trained to operate in spiritual things through the power of Jesus Christ. Josh McDowell believes that this will be the last Christian generation in our country if we do not act, the remnant generation the Bible talks about. Statistically we know that less than 4% of the children and young people under 30 years old are believers. This is war.

God's heart for today is we as teachers and parents, go to impart and to impact this next generation. We have been working and training for this. We are supposed to help them release their own anointing which they were born with. Bible stories are very important but children need to be equipped in the power of the Spirit. They need to have their own experience of the Holy Spirit, function in the gifts of the Holy Spirit and pray in the Holy Spirit, with power and authority.

"Listen, dear friends to God's truth, bend your ears to what I tell you. I'm chewing on the morsel of a proverb; I'll let you in on the sweet old truths. Stories we learned from our fathers, counsel we learned at our mother's knee. We're not keeping this to ourselves; we're passing it along to the next generation. God's fame and fortune, the marvelous things he has done. He planned a witness in Jacob; set His Word firmly in Israel. He commanded our

parents to teach it to their children, so the next generation would know them; and all generations to come would know the truth and tell stories to their children that they can trust in God. Never forget the works of God and keep his commands to the letter." (Psalm 78:1-7, MSG).

This has always been God's heart for each generation. This is God's heart for you today!

They tell us there were about three million Israelites when they left Egypt. These were hungry and thirsty people wandering through the desert complaining. That kind of complaining had to be intense. Anyone who has a hungry child knows what I am talking about. I can only imagine what Moses went through! I once heard that just to provide the minimum ration of food and water would have required thirty boxcars of food and three hundred tank cars of water every day—for forty years!

When the Israelites couldn't find water anywhere, they cried out to God for help. Jesus's disciples were no better because they cried out for help! The disciples did not even want the children to receive ministry but Jesus set them straight, *"Don't push these children away. Don't ever get between them and me. These children are at the very center of life in this place."* (Mark 10:13-14, MSG).

There were many miracles of provision. Twice, God even caused gushing springs of water to flow from a rock! God's people soon forgot what He had done for them because they had not learned how to meditate on God's past works. Because of this they lacked faith for their present needs.

Complaining is always a lack of faith. You can see they didn't understand this principal! *"Never forget the works of God and keep his commands to the letter. Heaven forbid they should be like their parents, bull headed and bad. A fickle and faithless bunch who never stayed true to God."* (Psalm 78:7-8, MSG)

Just think about it, there has never been a generation that has passed its revival to the next generation effectively.

We have a crisis in the present day body of Christ. As many as 70% of children who have been raised in Bible believing churches and families are leaving the organized church in droves by the time they reach their teens and young adult years, as reported by the Southern Baptist organization. What's worse is they never return. Research shows that by the time many children are thirteen years old they feel they know everything there is to know about the Bible and God, and feel no further need of attending church. Could this be because we have underestimated their spiritual potential, and have been content to feed them a repetitive spiritual diet of basic Bible stories over and over again? It's time the collective body of Christ re-evaluate children and youth ministries and redefine what valid, disciple-making, equipping children/youth ministry really is.

What is of interest is that George Barna recently reported:

"Fact: 47% of our youth, boys and girls alike lose their virginity on prom night.

Fact: Violence and abuse is at the forefront of the media on any given day or night. CNN reported just last week that a child is abused every ten seconds in America. The estimate is 3 million children but experts are saying the figure is 3 times that.

Fact: Today Focus on the Family reported children raised by homosexual parents are dramatically more likely than peers to suffer from a host of social problems.

Fact: There are 3,000 acts of sex presented to our young people weekly on national TV.

Fact: Today it is point and click porn. 90% of our children are on line by the time they are 7 years old."

There is a movement called the "Indigo Children." The basic premise is that these children are psychic and can see into the spirit realm. What the psychics have identified is the imitation of the real thing. Then we have Harry Potter, Digimon, Pokémon and the list goes on. The devil never created anything original. All he can do is try to counterfeit what God is doing.

In order to stand, children must develop:

- Passion for prayer and intercession in order to develop like Moses (Ex. 33:11) as one who spoke with God as a friend face to face. Or like Adam, who walked and talked with God in the garden. This is the place where children can find friendship, strength, wisdom, and an abundance of love. That is God's desire too. We must teach them how to practice hearing God's voice and being led by His Spirit. They must be trained to operate in spiritual things through the power of Jesus Christ. God wants us to love Him with all of our heart, mind, and soul, because He loves us with all of His heart, mind, and Spirit. Jesus wants us to love Him the way that He loves us. God's ultimate eternal purpose for creation is to provide a family for Himself that includes faithful children for Himself and an equally yoked Bride for Jesus eternally.

- Passion for His intimacy (Ex. 3:2-5). Moses was fascinated by God, His awesome presence, and His power, so he spent time there. He treasured God's presence. This is worship, pressing into the heart of God and having a real encounter with God.

    I prayed with a thirteen-year-old just the other night and asked, "What did you feel, what did you hear, what did God tell you?"

    He said, "I did not expect to feel or see anything but wow, wow, I never knew God was really real." It is only in His Presence that He releases His Power.

- Passion for war in order to be effective warriors

in God's kingdom. Paul said, *"in order that satan might not outwit us. For we are not unaware of his schemes."* (2 Corinthians 2:11, NIV). It's more important than ever that children can recognize the true from the false in our society, we must train them in what the Bible says about the spirit world. We must teach children to apply what they have learned.

We are truly in a spiritual battle over this generation, and as a result, God is pouring out His Spirit like crazy on those who will accept this shift in the Spirit. This generation was truly born ripe and ready for the pouring out of God's Spirit as spoken by the Prophets.

I can remember reading about a little girl in the early 1400 hundreds. She was a Holy Spirit filled girl we know as Joan of Arc who had the anointing so powerful that people often brought the sick and the dead to her. History remembers her as one who valiantly gave her country hope and from hope; victory after her two brothers had been killed in the Hundred Year War, claiming that God gave her the strategy. Vincent Milner claims in his book Religious Denominations of the World that children of five or six in the 1600's said they saw heaven opening up and they saw hell, they began prophesying and calling people to repentance and salvation. The Huguenots' reported young babies in orphanages singing in a foreign language. The Nuns called in French doctors who reported that the children were singing in a prayer language to God and he told the nurses to leave them alone. In 1707 John Wesley told of children who were three or four in trances convicted of sin having a powerfully deep experience with God, deeper than some of the adults. Jonathan Edwards reported very many children expressing themselves far beyond their years. D.L. Moody began his teaching with a revival in children and today we can expect the same for our children if we allow the Holy Spirit to lead. He says in the last days I will pour out my spirit so that our sons and daughters will prophesy.

God is serious! Satan is serious! We have to get serious! You have the opportunity to be a Shepherd as David was to the children/youth He has brought for you to mentor. Train up your own children in the ways of God to be mighty sons and daughters. As parents it is imperative for you to be proactive in their spiritual life. God bless each of you as you pray and prepare your hearts to serve the Lion of Judah in teaching children how to embrace the goodness of the Lord.

Chapter 2

Passion for Prayer and Intercession

HOW DO YOU KNOW IF YOU ARE HEARING GOD'S VOICE?

I have asked myself, why? Why me, God? There are so many who are so gifted and I am just me. Haven't we all said that about getting engaged with God? I have heard it said that we need to feel we are qualified, gifted in this or that, while the truth is we are no better off than Jesus disciples, John and Peter. They all had issues including Jacob, David, Noah, and Jonah. The point is, He is searching for those with willing hearts to hear His voice and just do it! The key is they said "yes" to the Lord. It is true God uses us in spite of ourselves.

I met my friend, Lenny LaGuardia, and it has been an adventure ever since. I gleaned so much at that first little conference in Kansas City. God was using Lenny to train missionary kids and the children who have parents in ministry. The conference was very small so it was easy to ask questions and interact with him and his staff. Little did I know at the time, we were both at the door of pioneering and sowing into new territories in the Spirit as it relates to children. By Sunday morning of the conference there were just a few of us, and he had us observe his teaching with his children. He had us all sit in a circle, the children stood behind us. He had the children pray and ask God for a word and each child came and laid a hand on my shoulder and spoke so clearly, words of encouragement, words that were edifying and words of comfort.

This one boy said, "I see two logs stretched across a valley and you are balancing on these logs trying to cross the valley. If you look down, you will fall. If you look back, you will fall.

God wants you to always look forward."

He was about ten! I remember going back to my room that night and crying out to the Lord that my desire for the children of our church was for ministry to flow in the Spirit like I had seen in Australia and now here. I had worked with another large children's ministry for years but never had I seen these kinds of results. I had not seen children who knew what it meant to love the Lord with all their heart, soul, and mind, who listened to His voice, and did what He told them to do.

I cried out to the Lord almost the whole way home asking, "how?" We had experienced it in Australia with missionary kid's and Lenny was imparting it in Kansas City with missionary kid's, but could it be done in a church? Could I do this? I knew it would have to be the Lord, for I was inadequate even though I had diplomas from two different schools of ministry. I was willing, no matter what it cost. Little did I know!

I went back, consumed with how to actually implement this change. There wasn't any curriculum for this sort of thing. I met with my pastor Alan DeBoer. He is an amazing man of God and has a gift to receive vision and encourage others to move in it. He, too, had a desire to see the children of our church moving in prayer and intercession. What pastor would not?

I met with my team, wondering if this radical shift would run them off. Some had been there longer than I had, and all were well trained in children's ministry, seasoned teachers. The program they had been doing was amazing with so much fun; puppets, drama, Hawaiian themes, Cowboy themes, techno, lots of games, and Bible trivia. It was good! I began to explain that I had been to this conference, where there was no curriculum and immediately I saw the look on their faces. I began to explain that things were shifting in the Spirit as it relates to children. God had been showing me about something in Malachi 4:6, *"And he shall turn the heart of the fathers to the children, and the heart of the children to their fathers, lest I come and strike the earth with a curse".*

All I knew to do was pray. That is what we had done in

Australia and that is what they were doing at IHOP. Our team met at 8am that first Sunday morning and I remember how frightened I was and yet full of zeal for the Lord. We prayed for about thirty minutes, asking the Lord to reveal His plan for this day; which of us was to teach, what we were to teach, for a heart of worship, and for a scripture. Then one by one as we shared, the Holy Spirit began to give us a plan. The children came in and we began with ice breaker games, and connected with worship, teaching, and prayer. Later we found out the adults had had the same scripture and message in church that morning! We knew we had nailed it! I never dreamed this could be done in a church setting but this was not about me!

And so we began this wild adventure with God and the Holy Spirit. Although I had worked with children for many years and had training as a children's pastor, my passion after mission training was to serve as a children's missionary. My pastor came to me when I returned from Australia and asked if I would consider coming on staff as Children's Ministry Director? I told him no. I felt my calling was to serve as a children's missionary, as I had done for years. He then asked if I would pray about it and meet with him in a week. I hate it when I have my mind made up and God has other plans. I was miserable the whole week as God dealt with me. Finally, I surrendered. It is about surrendering your own will, isn't it? Making Jesus Lord over everything is not always an easy thing. I met with my pastor and told him my heart and passion was missions; however, God had begun showing me that I could take the position. God told me I could train children with a heart and a passion for missions, and model that for them.

We got our little group together each Sunday morning, and to our amazement we would end up teaching what the adults had been learning next door. So many people constantly ask me, "How do you know you hear God's voice?" Those confirmations were powerful. The pastor and I would meet on Tuesday mornings and he would ask what we taught on and how it went. I never knew what his sermon was going to be but God did.

We began taking the kids to our local park on Wednesday afternoons with a boom box; worshiping, signing, testimony and teaching. We all loved it and felt we were really blessing God.

What we were doing without even realizing it was allowing Holy Spirit to develop a spirit of boldness in ourselves and in our children. *"When we trust in him, we're free to say whatever needs to be said, bold to go wherever we need to go."* (Ephesians 3:12, MSG).

Worship and 24/7 prayer is the whole premise of the International House of Prayer as well as with Youth with A Mission. *"Will God not bring about justice for His elect who cry out to Him in day and night prayer?"* (Luke 18:7). We were not trying to copy or mimic what was going on at IHOP, but God soon began to lead us in worship. We asked some of the worship leaders in our church if they would come and lead worship for the children, but like in many churches they were more interested in serving the adults. (After all, the adults control the finances and adults like to build relationships, right?) My team and I have come to believe the most important place for ministry is among the children. I know my friend and colleague, Lenny La Guardia, agrees. The big thing we learned from that experience is that whenever we needed help, we would simply pray and petition God, because He was showing us over and over that this was His ministry and not ours.

At this very moment, an entire generation of children and young people are at risk. Giant corporations, media conglomerates, and other purveyors of popular culture have leveraged every dollar they can spare, as well as every waking hour, into claiming the souls of today's children and youth. Indeed, God is showing us there is something bigger going on in the Spirit, a war, a battle raging!

It wasn't long before we dedicated one of our Sunday school rooms to only prayer. The kids named it the Children's Healing Room and one of the girls made a sign to that effect on a piece of wood painted purple with flowers on it and proudly hung it on the door. We added a CD player with worship going on 24/7. On Sundays, after our lesson, we would all crowd in there on the floor. The kids totally owned that room. There was no horsing around; they were serious. My friend Tammy brought her guitar and would quietly play while the children prayed for nations, for healing, for forgiveness, and on and on. We had one boy with

Down Syndrome and when he prayed, he became transferred. The Holy Spirit would rise up in him and you knew it was that the same Holy Spirit that lived in you as a kid. Didn't Moses stutter when not in the presence of God?

Children are God's arrows, which we are to sharpen. In Psalms we are told that the arrows are to be fired into the city gates. The city gates represent the places of authority, for it was where the elders sat.

Now is the time to prepare the children. We are supposed to bring them into the anointing. Bible stories are very important, but children need to be equipped in the power of the Spirit. They need to have their own experience of the power and presence of God. They need to be filled with the Holy Spirit, and taught how to operate in the anointing and gifts of the Spirit.

While I was ministering at a large conference in Central Asia for missionaries, I observed a family who would come in after the adults had finished worship. We had finished worshiping and were ministering to the children. This late arrival would stop the flow of the Holy Spirit. All the children would look up and that was it! Kids are just that way.

This family ministered in one of those places where they could easily have been martyred, so I won't tell you where. I talked to the Mom and asked her to please let her children worship with us because of the disruption to the other children when they arrived late. She explained that, because of their ministry location, it was not often that they could be with a large group, and experience the anointing. I tried to assure her that her children would be in the anointing. Our vision was in ministry to children, not to entertain them. She very reluctantly began sending her daughters on time. At the end of the conference, she and her husband came to me with tears in their eyes and thanked me. As a result of the ministry their daughters received they had begun moving in the prophetic with a prayer language. The Mother had told me they had never had anyone come to equip children in the power of the Holy Spirit. All they knew for ministry was games, stories, and puppets. I do not do puppets!

The same Holy Spirit is at work in the children as in the adults. I know there is not much a kid can do in the natural but in the anointing they are as powerful as anyone. Children can and do prophesy the Word, cast out demons, be powerful in intercession, lay hands on the sick and see them healed. With the children, we go deep and we go fast. They do not have all of the distractions we have as adults, their hearts are pure and ready for intimacy with God. Kids can be in the Spirit totally one minute and clobbering their brother the next. Jesus said, *"I praise you, Father, Lord of heaven and earth, because you have hidden these things from the wise and learned, and revealed them to little children."* (Matthew 11:25).

Prophecy is simply intimacy, the drawing near of God. God's desire is that we become like Him. He wants his people to be with Him forever. His desire is that we become one with Him, distinct, but like Him. Revelation is understanding our dependency on God. It gets in the way is our view of Him as a reflection of the way we were raised. Many of us have been raised with the idea that we cannot have intimacy with God because we are caught up in sin, we are not good enough, we do not measure up, or we are not knowledgeable of Biblical teachings. Many people think God is saying, "don't come near me until you get it right, don't even bother. Once you are good enough, you can draw near." This is just not true. God desires us to come to Him. God is already near; He wants us to press into Him. He will change in you what He wants changed. Intimacy produces passion. Press into God, draw near to Him. Prophecy is an overflow of intimacy. *"Jesus is the Spirit of Prophecy."* Revelation 19:10).

Chapter 3
Clean Fresh Water

PASSION FOR THE RIVER

Pastor Mike Bickle teaches that Intercessory prayer is intimacy. Prayer is an exchange of romance. God speaks to us and it moves our hearts. When we speak back to God, His heart is moved. God desires to establish or deepen this romantic relationship with us. He desires intimacy with us. He wants us to know His heart and more, to feel the very emotions of His heart, and then He wants to hear us cry out for the longings of His heart to come to pass. His longings become our longings. It's partnership at the most intimate level possible. We begin to feel and do what God feels and does.

I was asked by a pastor in Minnesota to facilitate a mission trip for some youth desiring to serve on an American Indian reservation. Our team met with the youth group in a nearby border town. As we started ministering that night I began to realize they were not as open to the power of God as the pastor had shared. I put my intercessors to work. These kids were crying out for God to change their (the youth from Minnesota) lives and strike their hearts so they could go deeper with God. Their team was first on the program that night doing a skit, puppets, and some signing to a worship song. One of our thirteen year olds preached and then led in praying individually for the people in the church. I was busy and did not notice what was going on until I heard, "Dude, you are on the floor!" Two of our boys, one nine and the other ten, were praying for a reservation pastor when he went out in the spirit. Our ministry time lasted a couple of hours with the kids doing the praying. The leaders and children from that ministry had a lot of questions for me after that night.

The next morning, I took our group to another native pastor's house where they were to paint his house. By afternoon the sky turned black and we began hearing thunder in the distance. I circled both teams in the cul-de-sac where the pastor's home was located, just as the pastor left for town to get more supplies. We prayed and interceded for God to show His power in holding back the rain until we had finished painting. When the pastor returned he was soaked. He said it rained so much in town that the Indian Ceremonial dance, which is always about animism, scheduled for that afternoon, was canceled. Too much rain! We, however, were in the middle of a circle of black clouds with beautiful blue sky above us, painting the pastor's house under an open heaven.

On the third day we took the kids on a thirty-minute hike to a high point on the reservation. There is a large natural kind of cave there where we could look out for miles, and we had planned to simply intercede for God's word to run swiftly over this reservation. The cave smelled a little musty after all the rain the day before. One of their girls began to have a severe asthma attack. One of their leaders was an RN and she expressed concern as we were miles from the nearest hospital. We began interceding for her and it was not long before she was able to breathe normally. The nurse said that even with an inhaler she had never seen anyone recover from such a bad attack so quickly. Needless to say, the team returned home changed by their own experience and a real touch from the Father. This was not something they could read about or experience in a three-point lesson plan.

These young people learned that intercession is a partnership. Intercession is the means by which God's will is established on earth. God does not act apart from human beings partnering with His heart. Intercession expresses the bridal identity of the church. There is nothing more powerful that can fuel God's heart to move upon the earth than the cry of His bride, whose desires reflect His own.

Intercession is agreement with what God promised to do. When we ask God to do what He desires, we are declaring that we agree that His desires are good, and that His desires have become our desires.

The church has so underestimated and undervalued

children's ability to readily accept and understand these principles. Children do not have a pint sized Holy Spirit; God is God no matter what our age and the same Holy Spirit who lives in us lives in our children.

Here is a little prayer guide I have adapted based on my teaching with Youth with a Mission, that is simple for children to understand. We begin our teaching on prayer by simply allowing the kids to talk to God, saying whatever is on their heart. After a few weeks as they have developed that heart, we teach several points and practice each one in this guide.

How to Pray:

- Praise God for who He is. Thank Him for allowing you to be part of His ministry. (Hebrews 7:25)
- Make a clean heart by asking God to help you remember what you need to ask forgiveness for. (Psalm 66:18-19, Psalm 139:23-24)
- Tell God you know you can't really pray without the direction of the Holy Spirit. (Romans 8:26, Ephesians 5:18)
- This is the time I choose to spend with my God and Savior, in the name of Jesus Christ. (James 4:7)
- Let God have your own thoughts and imaginations. (Proverbs 3:5-6, 28:26)
- Praise God for the prayer meeting that you are going to have with Him. Now be quiet and wait for God to tell you what you should pray for. (Psalm 62:5, Micah 7:7, Psalm 81:11-13)
- Speak out what you believe God has brought to your mind. (John 10:27, Psalm 32:8-9)
- You will need to have your Bible if God wants to give you a scripture. (Psalm 119:105)
- When you feel you have prayed what God told you to, thank Him for what He has done. (1 John 5:14-15)

Teaching these principles to children will give them a thirst for more of God. Pastor Bob Sorge at IHOP calls it a passion for the river. Pastor Sorge talks about the best drink of water he ever had (Rev. 22:1-2).

I can remember the best drink of water I ever had. It took place a few years ago in the mountains outside in a little village in a nation where Islam is the faith of the country. We had taken a bunch of kids up there for a time of ministry and camping. It was very hot and many children came to see the foreigners, many adults came bringing gifts of a fresh yogurt drink, warm with hair and dirt still in it! Yes of course, we drank it and believed the Holy Spirit would bless that which we were about to receive. Yes, there is a point to saying grace before a meal! I believe we were the first white people in that area as less than 1% of all mission work is done in Muslim countries. Most people are afraid to go to those hard places; sadly, most missionaries prefer the easier nations. God loves all people equally and we did not find it hard at all.

It was very hot and our last day, we had had no water since the night before. It was humid and we were all weary. As we traveled down the mountain in our van it was nice not to have to get out and walk and push the van uphill as we did going in. We passed a group of ladies stuffing their mattresses with the fresh grass hay and straw they had gathered and stuffed in a sack they carried on their backs down the mountain. We are so blessed in our country and do not even realize what others endure.

We had seen an artesian spring on our way up and were so glad to get there. The kids all went first satisfying their thirsts. I leaned over and took a long drink. The water was so clean and fresh and yet I could not get enough, it was so good."

This is the kind of thirst we are seeing in children today; they are thirsty for fresh water for their souls. American children are being raised in humanism. Humanism is a religion, the day begins and ends with me, what makes me feel good, how much more can I get. As the church, we have compromised. We have become tolerant and refuse to cause waves or stir things up. If you look at Jesus it seems to me He did not compromise. I have had some very good training in children's ministry and I know many games, cute songs and I can do puppets with the best of them, but I will not compromise.

Even though we are all good at dramatic Bible stories, games and puppets, I believe the missing ingredient in children's ministry has been our lack of understanding that children need that drink from the river, and that will begin to develop a passion for the river. Psalms 46:4 says that, *"There is a river whose city will make glad the river of God.*

The river is real and I believe children were created to drink from that river; it is their destiny. The real longings of their heart can only be satisfied through a passion for God.

I had a vision about a dead river surrounded by red sand. There was actually a sign that said, "Dead River." The Holy Spirit revealed to me that the red sand represented the blood of all the children who were so entertained that they never got to drink from the river of life.

All around the river I saw boulders, obstacles if you will, that were holding children back from the river, as they did not know how to get over or around those big boulders.

I then saw the things of the world that entertain our children, video games, television, sports, and I thought these things are not really bad in and of themselves.

I then remembered my grandson who would spend the day in front of the television unless someone made him turn it off. There are drugs, alcohol and sex all robbing children and youth of their destiny.

I then saw water beginning to flow in the stream and children beginning to overcome the boulders, and begin to get wet little by little and then become consumed by the river. That is what we are experiencing today, those of us who can hear and those of us who can see.

Ministry to youth and children is changing as children are being consumed by the Holy Spirit. Our prayer Father, is for a generation to be consumed by you.

Chapter 4
Don't Stop Until the Kids Do!

DEVELOPING A LOVE RELATIONSHIP WITH JESUS

-BY TAMMY SEARLE-

As you begin your adventure pouring into kids, teaching, training, and equipping, I advise you to stay light and push the easy button! Keep it fun and keep showing up! Exhale and push the easy button often! This simple practice is great to prevent over striving and burn out.

If you are going to sustain yourself in any ministry you have got to amp up your own personal walk and quiet time. If you look at men and women who have been in ministry for years, the first thing you see is a deep relationship with God which can only develop through spending time developing intimacy.

Get a group of precious prayer warriors covering you. Form a leadership team of like-minded forerunners who have a passion for raising up the end time saints. Seek strategy and direction from the Holy Spirit. Listen and obey.

Shortly after our commitment to run with this ministry on Sunday mornings and in the after school club, I had an idea to rally the kids and see if there might be an interest to form a children's church praise band. I love to sing, play my guitar and worship, so getting the kids encouraged in music and worship with their voices and instruments seemed like an easy and obvious "add on" to what we were already doing.

The response from the kids was encouraging; we had about fifteen to twenty little worshipers show up consistently, once a week, for months! I had taught my boys some basic guitar chords prior to our band gatherings, so we were the musicians and the other kids were singers, signers, and/or drummers. It was a crazy time.

Let me pause right here and honestly tell you I hadn't found my easy button at this point in time of this adventure of mentoring children! Staying light was not even in my vocabulary! With only two of us adults overseeing this effort each week, I will give you an idea of what early praise band practices were like.

First of all, I immediately started everyone out with microphones and instruments plugged into a sound system. Crazy idea, but the kids loved it! The church staff who had offices in the same building, well, not so much! I remember at least two of the younger worshipers being quite a hand full, and they required all of my assistant's time and attention. We look back and laugh now, at how Virginia was the behavior "heavy," Tammy was the "leader of the band." Visualize a lot of loud, not so skillfully played, worship songs blasting out of the monitors and speakers and a couple of boys running around turning the room upside down - for two hours!

Needless to say, I arrived home after these sessions a little frazzled and fried! One particular evening, after yet another crazy time of what we called praise band practice, my husband asked me, "Why do you keep doing this?" I replied, "I don't know."

The next week we showed up again, and then again, and again, and again. The kids were faithful to keep showing up too. They had a ball! This doesn't sound very spiritual, but I believe one of the reasons they kept showing up was because they were allowed to sing on microphones! "Just sayin'," keep it simple, keep it fun, and wear earplugs!

The small beginnings of this "season" progressed into kids leading kids in praise and worship during our Children's Church on Sunday mornings. Other kids were encouraged in their hearts of worship gifting. Other adults came along side to help! Kids developed a love for music and worship!

As of this writing, these same young worshipers are young

adults now, playing skillfully before the Lord, and ushering in His presence. What a blessing! What fruit! I've got easy buttons now, I exhale often, and I know exactly why I keep doing it!

I've yet to meet a child that didn't like to sing! Recently I have encouraged the after school club kids to meet through the summer months. We meet for an hour each week to worship and praise the Lord, primarily focusing on playing music, singing, prophetic dance, and drawing.

I find myself having flash backs to the early days of children's praise band practice. Pleasant flash backs I might add. Somehow the passing of time has eased the memory of those crazy early days. The little song birds and dancers that show up each week are a joy to sing and dance with before the Lord.

I'm convinced if you offer children a place to explore and express their musical and creative sides, and get the parents committed to taxi them regularly, they instantly can engage in pursuing what is the beginning of a lifelong love relationship with Jesus!

I had one Mom bless me with the testimony of what happens in their home when her daughter sings praises to God. As she shared with me, her voice quivered and her eyes became moist with tears. She described how the atmosphere in the house changes when her six-year-old daughter sings the songs that she learns.

These special highlights of Heaven invading earth in the midst of raising up the smaller saints are very encouraging to keep you going back week after week, and year after year! My prayer as you read this, is that you are gaining confirmation and insight into your calling to equip and train the younger ones. I want to end this chapter with one more story that is sure to inspire you!

I found the very post that I made to my prayer warrior intercessors the day after we had experienced an awesome time of worship with the children. I can't reword it any better than I did that day, so I put some "copy and paste" computer magic to it and here it is…

"Hello awesome prayer warriors,

I want to share with you how your prayers are being answered.

Yesterday before arriving at the elementary school for our Jelly Beans and Squiggly Things Afterschool Club I'm encouraged with the plan to press in with praise and worship and read a Bible story with the kids, that's it!

Typically, over the past 10 years I've planned way more to do in the club than is even possible in the time that we have. To only have two things on my "lesson plan" for the day felt "refreshing" in my spirit. (Did I ever tell you about my deliverance experience from STRIVING!!!)? At about 3:50pm we started singing.

The Holy Spirit gave me the song that sings Revelation 1:14, John's physical description of Jesus and the kids love it. We sang it a lot last year during our 6-week Revelation study.

A few of my future worship leaders hop up and lead the hand motions as we're singing along, having a great time, everyone is engaged and the Holy Spirit gives me some "tags" (short one-liners to add onto the song). The kids catch right on and I become aware of a "shift" in the room, the volume of their voices begins to increase, in a good, loud way! I am aware especially as they sing "Jesus!" repeatedly 12-16 times! I get an open vision of this increased volume level of this melodious "Jeeeesssuusss" flowing out the door and into the hallways of the entire school! The kids are singing their hearts out! Soon about twenty minutes have passed and the thought goes thru my head, "wow, they are really getting after this!" I hear the Holy Spirit say to me, "don't stop playing and singing until the kids do!" Cool! Works for me!

The kids are just going for it; the Spirit of the Lord is upon them!!! Some are doing hand motions, some have their eyes closed and are singing Jesus, Jesus, Jesus! I actually experience watching the countenance on their sweet faces change and they just keep going, and going and going.

One of my leaders shows up to the club about twenty-five minutes into this and nobody "misses a beat". I see Ryan's eyes get wider and an expression comes over his face that nonverbally says "wow, check this out!" He pulls out his IPhone and starts to video this revival fire!

I'm choking back tears by now and can only play my guitar, it's hard to sing when you're crying, so I get a "blast blessing" of hearing angelic voices praise Him! This "throne room praise" continues for another twenty minutes, the kids are able to stay in this attitude of praise and begin speaking out prayer requests, for sick siblings and three different children pray for mom and dad to get back together. My leaders pray to "seal it" in the kid's hearts what they just experienced while in the presence.

Two little girls had visions while praising; one said that she saw Jesus walking around the room and she motions to Him. She demonstrates to me how she used the nonverbal, universal sign with her forefinger that "reads,"...come here! Jesus came over and sat down with us!

I did a mini debrief with the kids, which by now are STILL in a quiet, peaceful place in their heads and hearts, of how they just experienced being with Jesus and can go there often, to take it back to their homes, pray for mom and dad, and sing, sing, sing!

Thank you so much for your prayers! We had two new kids come to Jelly Beans and Squiggly Things Afterschool Club this day and they received Jesus! What can I say it was an "over the top" day, unlike any I've ever experienced in 11 years. The bar has been raised".

Are you encouraged? Do you now have a fresh vision for mentoring children without a curriculum? Be encouraged, you can do this! Follow the promptings of the Holy Spirit and keep showing up! Get a prayer covering and communicate often with them. Have fun, and remember, don't stop until the kids do!

Chapter 5
Engaging Feelings to Feel Better

"BE STILL AND KNOW THAT I AM GOD"

I think it is easy for kids to move in the prophetic. The Word says, "All can prophesy." Here are some of the things I have heard and recorded from children over the years, most between the ages of five to thirteen:

- There is a treasure chest full of people. God was so bright; you couldn't see His face. God shines the light of the world as it shines on the chest which holds His riches, His people are His riches.
- I saw a city in the road and the road is cracked and all non-believers in the road are falling in the cracks and the only people standing were saved people.
- Jesus on the throne and spirits around him were rich with people.
- I saw a dove bringing the message that it is God's world and that is the message to the whole world.
- The future is at the pearly white gates of heaven not on the road to God. It's a map and the road leads to the flood light, God.
- God's light flooding your heart.
- Without Jesus, you really don't have light. Jesus light begins to shine in you but you still have your eyes closed. Jesus light begins to shine as you keep sitting in the light and your eyes are open now. You want to share what Jesus has shown you.
- I saw a sand castle and God's people holding back

- the walls, and satan's army is crumbling.
- I felt the Holy Spirit. I had someone pray over me and I felt God.
- I felt the power of God and wanted to talk about Him. I knew my heart got unlocked.
- I heard God say, "you are beautiful, I love you no matter what."
- I was looking at the stars; a star looked like a key going into your heart.
- I saw the devil; he was standing with nothing but dry bones behind him. God was with the angels, who had trumpets, and they blew the trumpets and dry bones came alive and the people went to God's side.
- Another voice said that we were spiritual scouts, next comes the army.

Of course there are many more but hopefully you get the idea. A person just can't make this stuff up!

I Corinthians 14:3 says, *"but he who prophecies speaks edification, exhortation and comfort to men."* When we edify someone we simply build them up, to engage their feelings to feel better about things or themselves. For instance, when we tell a child that God is proud of them for being kind, honest, or generous, they are encouraged and this builds hope and faith. Now that he knows God is proud of him, he is encouraged and begins to realize that God really does love him. It frees him and he is happy.

We like to have children sit across from each other and then ask each to get a word for the person sitting across from them. Now kids will usually sit with their friends so the one sitting across is not usually a close friend and they sometimes giggle at the idea of getting something good for that peer. I remember this very young boy sitting across from a much older girl. He began, "I see roots of a bush and they are growing deep below the ground... the bush is a rose bush and the roses are dark purple but one is open and very pretty." Once we got, "hold your ears so that all He hears is your praise." "Jesus loves you" is a prophetic word for a child or an adult.

Exhortation is a big word for a child or even a teen, so we like to say the word exhortation is simply a way of telling someone to press into God, or to draw near, some would say. It is really a word of encouragement, which is what the Holy Spirit really does. The child begins to understand that God, the Holy Spirit, lives in him and is with him all the time. Holy Spirit desires to help us grow. Our words are powerful and we can help others to come closer to God. A boy about ten years old spoke out at one of our sessions and said, "We are supposed to pray for Lacy, she told God she would do anything for Jesus." She was so blessed and encouraged by this. Today she is serving God in an Asian country. Our words are so powerful and children are so ready to receive the love and attention from God. They love to do this, to be still and listen to God. They love the feeling of connecting with Him.

This generation is so filled with media it is hard for many to *"Be still and know that I am God."* But even the most ADD kid in your group will appreciate this teaching and learn to be a blessing to the other children. I remember that our team would cringe when this one seven-year-old boy would come in. When we saw his Mother bringing him, the first thing I did was put my intercessors to praying or the boy and for our team. Little by little it wasn't long before I figured out when I was teaching, and he was there with me, teaching, and coaching him; He loved to preach. Soon we would go into a time of being still before God and he was there! I believe these kind of kids are meant to teach and preach.

So many children and youth today are filled with sadness, fear, and loneliness and are really hurting because of family situations, divorce, and on and on. The significant thing is that when we bring a word of comfort to someone they are again encouraged and they begin to cheer-up. Prophecy tells that child or teen something that only God knows about him.

We were doing a little exercise in the prophetic with some children at risk not too long ago. Half of the children and youth were lined up around the room with their eyes closed; the others sneaked up and laid their hand on the shoulder of the one with his eyes closed. Everyone was very still and quiet, the child with the closed eyes was to be still and ask God for a word to say to the other child. Two members of our team got basically the same word for one particular girl during the two times we did the exercise, not knowing who was behind them. One of the prophetic speakers even said he was not sure if it was a boy or girl behind him but he felt strongly that the word was for a girl. The word was, "God wants you to know that He thinks you are beautiful, that you have value, and right now you are feeling like no one loves you but God says that is a lie from satan. You are his and he never lies. You are beautiful." The other word for her was pretty much exactly the same. The first time it was spoken she sheepishly grinned. The second time this was spoken about her, you could see her spirit rise up in confidence, yet she was weeping, overcome with knowing God had spoken to her.

Later I learned that she was a twin, and Mom had taken the other twin home and left her there in the children's home. My heart cried and rejoiced for her; this was confirmation that God spoke just for her by using two different people to tell her something only God would know.

We are not telling the future. What we are doing is listening to God's voice and speaking what He has told us. A prophet is someone with a special calling. We do not even try to go into that realm with children. We never want to scare a child by telling him something like he is going to be a missionary to someplace or an intercessor. If we see something like that, we simply say, "God showed me that you really like to talk to Him or you like to tell others about Jesus."

We never have to point out any of the negatives; kids know what is wrong in their situation. God is always good and as a result always has good, loving, encouraging, and kind things to say to children. He does not embarrass children. Kids sometimes have a hard time believing the good things. We simply speak God's thoughts and ideas that the Holy Spirit has given to us for this person. Our goal is to engage their feelings with God's feelings. It might feel like it is us, but trust that it is God.

Chapter 6

Who Said You Can't Dance?

EXPRESSING OUR HEARTS UNTO THE LORD

Sometimes when God gives so much it is hard to put into words.

One time I was in Washington DC, and we were ministering to around 200 kids from all over the country. There was this one beautiful little girl who had cerebral palsy really bad. She was waiting for her healing to manifest. She was small for an eight-year-old, and had no control over her little arms, and her fingers were just barely there. Both her legs were in braces. Her Mom explained to me she had very weak muscles in her arms and her Dad quickly encouraged her Mom that she was ok, and God would deal with her needs. Wow!

Somehow, in spite of her disabilities, she managed to get her little arms together, and her hands, palm side up, waiting and asking for God to touch her. At one point we were all dancing to a worship song. She was real fidgety and she wanted me to get her up out of her chair and onto her feet. She stood there, braces locked tight not moving with tears streaming down her little face. I asked if she was ok. She said, "Yes, I am dancing," with a smile on her face. I could see it in the Spirit, God is so good.

There is Biblical basis for dance in scripture:

- Miriam took the tambourine and danced with all the women following her, it was a time of jubilee and thanksgiving. (Exodus 15:20)

- Halal is a Hebrew word meaning; to celebrate or rejoice, to praise, to shine, to be foolish. God wants us to see that dance helps us overcome our fear and stirs up our faith and our hope. The Lord has called us to battle like King Jehoshaphat, to recognize that dance drives back the forces of darkness. It is a radical act of worship, and as we worship God, He uses us to defeat the enemy. (2 Chronicles 20:21-25)

- David danced before the Lord with all that he had in humility. He loved the Lord with his whole heart and wanted to thank the Lord for His goodness and faithfulness. (2 Samuel 6:14)

- King Hezekiah appointed those who should praise in the gates of the Lord. (2 Chron. 29:30)

- Everything seems to turn to joy as we dance before the Lord. (Psalm 30:11) As an act of worship we are told to praise God with dance, for the Lord takes pleasure in His people. (Psalm 149:3-4)

- In the gospel of Luke, we see the prodigal son return home and so begins the dance of the lost that are found. (Luke 15:25)

It is easy for children/youth to follow a leader in dance, usually one of the older girls or sometimes a young one. We encourage them to simply lift up and glorify God through dance as an expression of our hearts to our God.

There is a Biblical basis for dance as an expression of our hearts unto the Lord for intercession, deliverance, and healing. You will witness the anointing fall on children as they dance. You will see deliverance, although we do not emphasize it, we do recognize sometimes there is a time and a place for it but in a group setting it is amazing what happens. *Where the spirit of the Lord is there is the freedom to break the chains that holds us in bondage.* (2 Corinthians 3:17)

- The anointing of Holy Spirit. (Isaiah 10:27)

- Deliverance and healing is brought forth through dance. (Luke 4:18)

- Everything we do we are to do as unto the Lord. (Romans 11:36)

- We are commanded to present our bodies a living and holy sacrifice to the Lord. (Romans 12:1-2)

Children love so easily; the act of pure worship is easily achieved. There is a strong Biblical basis for the pure worship of those who love the Lord.

- We are to bring glory to God in the way we dress. The priest wore holy garments when he ministered in the Holy of Holies. In the New Testament we are called priests and we are not to call attention to ourselves. The clothes we wear should not cause anyone else to stumble. Our purpose is to glorify and honor our Savior and our King. This is why it is important to wear our best. (Exodus 39, 1 Timothy 2:8-10, 1 Corinthians 10:31, Romans 14:13-23)

- We are to dance rightly before God with a pure heart. In the New Testament, Herodias's daughter used dance to bring evil to get what her mother wanted, which was John the Baptist, dead. In everything we think, say, and do, we need to be careful that our hearts and minds are pure. (Mark 6:22)

- We are to worship with a pure heart as an acceptable offering. It is important for children to have some teaching on repentance before dancing. We do not dance as the world dances, because we dance the dance of the redeemed saints. Romans 12:1-2

- We need right attitudes too; we are not man pleasers, but God pleasers. (Colossians 3:23-24)

God is worthy of all of our praise, using our whole body, our mind, our will, our emotions, our arms in thanksgiving, our fingers to play on instruments, our voice to shout to the Lord, to sing, to bow before Him, to be foolish, to celebrate.

We begin to understand how much we are loved by God and how He delights in us, His friend and His children, we can respond through our bodies and our hearts.

When things get hard we can sneak off to our rooms, put on some worship music and dance before our Lord. This is interceding; this is celebrating, warring in the spirit, and expressing our hearts unto the Lord and as God takes control our emotions will change. Teach these things to your children, better yet, model these things. These are good lessons for all children. It is not easy to be a child today.

Chapter 7

Passion for War

UNLOCKING YOUR HEART TO DEEPER THINGS

Disaster strikes the southern kingdom of Judah without warning, just as in the days of Joash. God is calling His Joel 2 Army in this day. CHILDREN/YOUTH ARE PART OF GOD'S JOEL 2 ARMY! Disaster has stricken this generation. A black cloud is covering this generation; locusts in the name of abortion are killing this generation, along with bad movies, bad language, and bad video games, lying and fighting. Many in our country have turned away from God. Many young people do not have homes and one and a half million children do not have parents. Joel was God's spokesman in his day. You are God's spokesman during this time on earth. You are to help prepare the planet for the coming of Jesus, He is coming again soon.

God blessed Noah and his sons, and God desires to bless you in everything. God says you were blessed when you were born. God desires to prosper you, for you to reproduce followers of Him, to build His army around the world. Every person belongs to God, and He longs for you to understand, and not only share your faith, but to come alongside other boys and girls, and to encourage that person God has put in your group of friends and family. Your responsibility is to live a Holy life; not only at home but everywhere you go. Holy simply means to surrender yourself completely to God by showing and teaching others what it is to live a cut above, your heart unlocked to the deeper things of God. This is making Jesus Lord of your life.

The children of Israel were led to the holy land by Moses after their escape from Egypt sometime around 1250 BC. Around 874-852 BC King Ahab became the seventh King to rule the Hebrew people. He was quite a guy, doing *"More evil in the sight of the Lord than all who were before him."* The Pharaoh of Egypt was the worst enemy of the Hebrews but now it seems to be the Philistines. The Philistines were not interested in God but more in themselves and having what others had (today we call that humanism).

King Ahab was influenced by the Philistines and his wife Jezebel. Jezebel was a priest of the fertility goddess, Astarte. She worshiped the false god, Baal. She had great influence over Ahab, and through her pressure and control, he soon began turning to idols and the worship of the forces of nature.

Ahab allowed the construction of temples and altars to honor Baal. He allowed the sacrifice of his own son, he also allowed alters of God to be destroyed, and he abandoned the laws of God. Ahab falsely accused people who opposed him, even killing some because all he wanted was control.

The prophet Elijah was not afraid to challenge the priests of Baal. Elijah was the greatest enemy of Ahab and Jezebel because he was a godly man.

On one occasion Elijah worked a miracle of calling down fire from heaven.

Ahab was tireless in doing evil things and he suffered some serious consequences because of disobeying the Lord. We, too, suffer consequences when we do not obey God and choose things we know are wrong or false.

Today, kids are so bombarded by distractions that become stumbling blocks to steal their time with God. It is more important than ever for kids to know and understand Godly principles and values as it relates to them. They need to know that lying is wrong, cheating on tests is wrong, along with, bullying, swearing, abortion, premarital sex, homosexuality, anger, depression, focusing on just themselves, these things are considered wrong concepts as it relates to following God.

Do not misunderstand me, for I hate legalism! We teach children that all of these things are not of God, so they either choose to follow the Holy Spirit or an unholy spirit. If children develop wise concepts, it will help to sustain them when it comes to peer pressure. I can say this with confidence because we have seen it over the years with the children we have worked with. Do not allow your children to open doors to the tactics of the enemy.

Following God's Holy Spirit- **TRUE**	Following an unholy spirit- **FALSE**
Being bold in expressing your faith in God, expressing what is true and good.	Being hopeless, mean, lying to those around you whether friends or family.
Showing respect for other people, parents, other family members, friends, teachers, people who serve you in stores or restaurants.	Just caring for yourself, being big headed, or being annoying to other people, family members, teachers, friends.
Willing and wanting to learn all you can.	Being a know it all, not listening.
Mighty through God, pressing into God, hearing His voice and doing what He tells you.	Being stubborn, standing your ground to prove you are bigger, stronger, and know everything.
Wanting to stay away from anything you know would not please God like bad movies, bad language.	Being cruel or mean, nasty or violent towards other people or animals. Doing things you know that are bad.
Surrendering to those in authority even when you do not want to clean your room or lay down a video game, etc.	Acting out or trying to get your own way in a situation by yelling or screaming in order to be in control.

Focused on God's agenda like reading your Bible, worship and prayer.	Always focused on ME and what I want with friends, school and at home.
A team player.	Never a team player always about ME.
Pure, real, innocent by choosing to look and listen to that which is good.	Thinking you are better than anyone else.
Understand and know that God says you were blessed when you were born, that you are His child and His friend.	Feelings like you are not as good, that you are not as nice looking, that your clothes are not good enough, jealous.
Fear of the Lord simply means to have awesome respect for the Lord.	Not knowing the Lord, you have no respect, and you make fun of Him.
Be wise in your decisions and the courage to achieve your goals.	You make fun of others to get them to do what you want them to do.
Share with your friends and family the truth about God.	Forcing others to do what you want out of fear.
Help other leaders in your church, school, community and your home.	Crush someone's feelings because they will not do what you want.
Being kind helps you to win or be successful.	Sometimes you win by cheating but no one really likes you because of it.

It is important for you to understand who really lives in you is God the Holy Spirit

Chapter 8

Dude, Just Kick Satan in the Butt!

TALKING TO OTHERS ABOUT YOUR LOVE FOR GOD

Life is a jungle out there and the mossies' are out to suck my blood! Why did God make mosquitoes anyway? How many insects do you think God created? God spoke everything into existence and when God spoke, he created 17-30 million insects in one verse! (Genesis 1:24) Ever hear a mosquito just before he bites you? Graham Cooke teaches "that is because every insect and every person is like a tuning fork in the spirit and each one of us has a certain sound that God always hears. That is why when you pray God always hears *you*!"

Like the mosquito, you were made for blood! The key is all in understanding who you are and what you are created for. It is important for you to understand who really lives in you is God the Holy Spirit, and He is there to be a partner, your strong tower, you will find your power in Him. Today that power belongs to you because of the blood Jesus shed on the cross. Jesus knew the power He needed here on earth could only be found coming from the Father. (Matthew 22:37, Mark 12:30, Luke 10:27, Psalm 61:3, Ephesians 5:18, John 5:19)

Jesus could not heal the sick. Jesus said it himself, "The Son can do nothing." He did perform signs, wonders, and miracles, as a man in a right relationship or a right connection to God. Jesus was a man who was confident of His link to God the Father. Jesus came to earth from heaven as a man because He knew that God is 100% good and that He always keeps His Word. He knew that if He asked God according to His Will He would give it to Him. Understanding the truth changes everything. Jesus asked God for His power before He could do anything. (Acts 2:22, John 5:19)

We all know that in the beginning God created the heavens and the earth. Man was created in God's image and God told Adam and Eve that His gift to them was the earth and they were to take over the earth. That was to be their mission field. That was God's plan and purpose for their lives. (Genesis 1:28, Genesis 1:2, Jeremiah 29:11)

He intended for them to have children, to choose to live by God's rules, and expand the Garden of Eden to the rest of the world. The more people who believed in Him, the better the earth would be. You don't have to be a rocket scientist to know that when you are living your life trying to be happy, thankful, obeying those in authority and submitting to God everything in your life is better. (Psalm 115:16, Romans 6:18)

Adam and Eve made a bad choice to go against what God had told them and by doing so they gave satan the opportunity to influence them. A big problem we face now was the same problem that Adam and Eve had. Temptation or peer pressure! (Genesis 3:2, Romans 3:23.)

Satan rebelled, and definitely did not want to be under God's authority and God kicked his butt out of heaven along with some angels who agreed with him, and they were sent to earth. So while Adam and Eve lived in the Garden of Eden and walked and talked with God, there were parts of the earth where things did not go so well because of the influence of darkness, or satan. You see the angels who left with satan, also known as demons, are always fighting, always upset, always mean, always lying, always cheating, always bullying, always doing bad things because they are just always bad. (Luke 10:18-20)

God's plan for man to rule the earth was taken away because Adam made the wrong choice. God could have destroyed the devil with a word, but He chose to stick to His plan to defeat the devil through men and women who would make the choice to love God with all their heart, soul, mind, and strength. Because God had given the rule of the earth to a man, the only way it could be taken back was by a man. The plan was that Adam would be that man. That is why Jesus came to earth as a man.

So you see, God's plan never really stopped. His plan for Adam is the same plan He has for you and for me. His plan is that you would always be close to Him and love Him. His plan is also that you would be a good influence in the earth. Jesus came to die for your sins and recapture what had been given away when Adam messed up and gave control of the earth to satan.

Just before Jesus died on the cross, He fasted for 40 days, and satan tried to ruin God's plan again. The devil knew he was not worthy of Jesus's worship. Satan knew Jesus had come to take away his power over you and me.

Satan said to Jesus, "if you will worship me, I will give you back the keys to the earth." He tried to trick Jesus! Jesus probably told him he was on a mud slide to hell! This is what we call peer pressure today. Jesus knew not to believe satan because He knew it was God the Father's desire satan would be defeated by a man, one made in God's image.

The book of Revelation is all about what the church and Jesus do to the devil. It is about us learning to move things out of the way, so Jesus can come and take control of the whole earth. God promised Jesus that He would rule all the nations. Today, the majority of the earth does not obey Jesus; when God promised Jesus the nations, He was talking about the people, not the land in the nations. Most of the nations that existed when Jesus walked the earth do not exist today as far as boundaries and land. When Jesus returns back to earth He is bringing heaven to earth and everything bad is going to go away.

We are to influence our friends and neighbors by sharing what our faith really means to us. The Bible says to let our light shine before men. Why? When we are silent about our faith we choose to keep people away from knowing God. When we talk to others about our love for God we give them the opportunity to be saved. Satan hates that! It kicks his butt!

Chapter 9

The Only Book

BE BOLD IN TEACHING YOUR CHILDREN TRUTH

1. The Only Book

I used to have a book; *Spiritual Battle Plan* written by a man named Humphrey; no relation. He says basically that satan does not want you to study the only Book in the world that can equip you with Karate. It is like don't think you can read like just one verse one time, take all of ten seconds to do it, and then think—I got it! I've got power! No, you don't! How long did it take to learn to tie your shoes? You have to get real close to God or press into God so He can show you how to unleash the awesome power of Holy Spirit in you. If you spend less than 10 seconds a day studying the word, and applying it or once a week on Sunday, you are not going to learn what the Bible offers. It is a choice to spend time in the Word. Learn the Bible so you can speak His Word—quote it to God and speak the Word of God to your own soul. Here are some simple words you can learn and speak to yourself each morning.

"The most important thing about me is that my name is _____ and God has plans for my life. I am His special child and I am completely accepted in Him. I am made by God and for God and He loves me, just as I am. The Holy Spirit lives in me. Nothing can separate me from the love of God. With His deepest love, God thinks about me all the time. I am created for good works. I am a friend of God. I thank you Jesus for the truth of who I am. I declare this in Jesus name."

Copy this and paste it on your bathroom mirror, or put it in your notebook so you see it every morning and every night. Things are really going to change for you once you believe this simple truth. Try it, what have you got to lose? (Jeremiah 29:11, 1 John 3:1, Ephesians 1:6, 1 Corinthians 3:16; 13:4, 7-8, Romans

8:14-15, 38-39, John 3:16;15:15, 2 Corinthians 5:17)

2. Rocket Worship

God is so creative that He made you in a unique and special way to easily connect with you through Christian music. The biggest part of your worship and praise should be connecting to God. We have many different songs in worship so that God can speak to each of us. What is your favorite worship song? When you connect with God in your praise, it is like a rocket! Jesus comes immediately to destroy anything around you that is not from heaven. God creates an atmosphere around you to give you His peace, His joy, and His love. Of course some music does not teach you the way to connect with God. When you choose to listen to your favorite worship music all day and at night it is like you open the door to heaven. God will continually bless you and speak to you. A good thing to do is simply put on a worship song, and hit repeat, and just soak and let the Holy Spirit wash over you. I love to do this when I am in my room, I just close the door, and dance, or lie on the floor and just listen.

My worship song is always on my heart especially when I am afraid because the enemy cannot stand in praise.

3. Burn the Enemy; Get Closer to the Flame

I teach this to the youth but it can apply to all ages. Walk daily in an attitude of letting Jesus lead you. Sometimes it seems like the things going on all around are just lame, people are angry, or afraid, your friends are mean, your Mom is sad, your teacher is really grumpy, your parents are getting a divorce, you are moving. You get the idea! My grandson Brandon is a wrestler, and he knows if he gets dazed, he has to get himself into a counter blow to his opponent, because he does not want to get pinned to the floor. That is where the enemy wants you, right? The Bible says the enemy comes to kill, steal, and destroy our destiny. All you have to do when things become difficult is to say, "Jesus replace those lies with your Truth," or if you can't remember that just say "Jesus, Jesus, Jesus" over and over. We have to use the name of Jesus in a place of warfare. Jesus has

Here we are interceeding for you. Our prayers won't stop being shot at your heart.

— Zach Bramble

WORSHIP AND PRAYER ARE THE KEYS TO AN OPEN DOOR TO HEAVEN

the authority to make the bad feelings or anything bad going on to stop. That is His power in you and His love for you. That is God, the Holy Spirit living in you. The enemy cannot stay where the name of Jesus is spoken. This is why your choice in music needs to be Christian music, God can speak to you as you listen, you stomp on the enemy's feet through worship and you learn more about God. (Proverbs 3:5-6, Psalms 34:4, 138:2, Luke 10:19, Romans 16:20, Zechariah 10:5)

4. Contact—Continue Kicking

Satan said to Adam, "Come on Adam, it is just one piece of fruit, no one will ever see you." But what happened? Adam knew it was wrong and he felt guilty, because all of a sudden his conscience kicked in and he ran to hide his nakedness. He tried to hide from God! When God asked Adam where he was it wasn't because God didn't know! We do the same thing. We tell ourselves, it is just one cookie, one swear word, one hit, but we know it is wrong immediately. We try to hide it! Sin is like dog poop! It is smelly, dirty and just plain yuck! If you get it on your hands, the first thing you want to do is wash it off so you are clean again. You can do that with God. As soon as you know something is not right you can kick satan in the butt simply by stopping and saying, "Father God, I was wrong. I am sorry, please forgive me. I love you." That is it! If you are sincere you are forgiven. (Joshua 1:8, Psalm 119, Ephesians 6:17)

Each one of us has that certain, unique sound that God always hears. That is why when you pray God always hears you! It is not about how you are feeling, but who you are. Because you are a child of God, things happen when you ask for forgiveness.

When God made Adam and Eve we are told in Genesis 1:28, "God blessed them." So it is for you, you are already blessed, you were born blessed. You are His child and you can receive all that the Father has. So every blessing you read about in the Bible is for you simply because you are His child. Your Father is a King, the Lord God Almighty, King of Kings, and Lord of Lords. Grab hold of that idea.

Here are some ideas to help you and the children you are

ministering to:

1. Read your Bible 1 minute a day for each year of your age. If you are 10, read the Bible for 10 minutes. Get the Message Bible it is great reading for a kid or a new believer.

2. If you have to read 20 minutes each night for school, read your Bible instead of some fiction book like Harry Potter. Let's take a quick detour here for one minute and see how Harry Potter and things like Pokémon line up with God's Word. The "psychic powers" teach young people to depend on supernatural powers and a spiritual source. Just because these powers are labeled good does not mean they are. Many in the entertainment industry and game industry have lied to you and told you it is okay to take part in them. You begin to believe it is okay to cast spells, and perform magic, but the Bible says in Deuteronomy 18 something like this, (in my words), "Don't fool around with things like fortunetelling, castings spells, holding séances, witchery or talking to the dead. The Bible says God thinks that is awful, dreadful and offensive." Your mind will begin to focus on what God hates, rather than on things God loves.

3. If you play video games, or watch TV for 30 minutes then give God 30 minutes by reading His Word, or go to your room and worship. Put on a worship song and hit repeat and just soak in the words and let the Holy Spirit wash over you, or dance before the Lord.

4. Riding in the car is a good place to read your Bible and it will make the trip go faster. Down load it on an iPod or iPhone and listen.

Chapter 10

Meaningless Colors and Numbers

MAKE IT SIMPLE, KEEP IT SPIRITUAL

Often, when we pray for children or even adults we ask them what God has done for them, what God has shown them, what did they see and hear when in the presence of the Holy Spirit. At the time of questioning, I immediately begin asking the Lord for an interpretation of what I am being told, and usually by the time they finish explaining, God has already given me the interpretation. He will do it for you as well and thus we experience signs, wonders and miracles. Isn't this what Jesus meant when He said they would follow us? Sometimes though, if it is quite a lengthy explanation, I will either ask the child or adult I am speaking with, to write it out. Sometimes I ask if I can pray more before offering an interpretation. I just want to give a clear interpretation based on hearing God's voice. If I am uncertain then I know I have not heard it from God. After all, it is not my job or responsibility, it is God's and He has never failed me.

God is so creative and imaginative; I find that there are really no set rules to encourage Him to do this or that according to what we think it should be. It seems to me that He is constantly doing things in different and new ways when we least expect it. I find this fascinating with God. It is great to be in constant prayer, longing to see just how He is going to move. God is not always logical, or maybe He is rubbing His hands with glee just to keep us in an atmosphere of anticipation.

Throughout your ministry to youth, many times children will say they have seen colors, or even numbers, and I won't try and interpret this for you, because once again it is the job of Holy Spirit to speak to you. Adopt the practice of Moses. Simply wait and pray; God will give you the meaning as it relates to each particular child.

If your desire is to see your children operate in the power of Holy Spirit, then you have to learn that kind of dependence as well. For so many years, youth ministry has been all about a curriculum, a designated teaching. My desire is for God to break in and mess up all of my plans! To Him be the Glory, and Honor, and Praise. It is not about us; it is all about Him.

God taught us in the very beginning that art belongs to Him, *"In the beginning God created..."* (Genesis 1:1)

The meanings of numbers are given throughout the scriptures such as the number one is related to the beginning, God, source of all unity, and control as mentioned in the books of John and Isaiah. The number seven is mentioned in Genesis, Matthew, and Revelation as completeness, perfection, days of rest, being finished, it is a sacred number. You must let God lead you on this interpretation. There are many numbers, please turn to the scriptures when attempting to find the meaning of numbers in dreams.

Simply, from what I have seen with children over the years, I will suggest some ideas God has given me as it relates to colors. Obviously, scripture has to be the basis, and it is all meaningless, as we know, unless Holy Spirit gives you the interpretation.

- **Red** often represents the Sacrifice. The fact that Jesus willingly surrendered himself on the cross or He took your punishment on the Cross. Red could also mean fire, war, courage, murder, judgment, love, life, death, but the Lord has to be the one to lead you into revelation as it relates to each individual child. (Red is spoken of in Genesis, Leviticus, Isaiah, Revelation, Joshua, and Hebrews.)
- **Blue** may represent the heavenly, or being seated with Jesus in heavenly places, the Holy Spirit, healing, the prophetic, grace, revelation,

knowledge, healing, or the priesthood. (Exodus, Numbers, Ezekiel)
- **Black** may represent death to self, a hiding place, sin, shadow of His Wings, evil omens, curses, affliction, mourning, humiliation, famine, distress, or suffering. (Lamentations, Malachi, Jeremiah, Psalm, Ephesians, Revelation.)
- **Yellow or Gold** represents light, joy, celebration, glory, counsel of God, revealed and could have to do with deity, wealth, kingliness, refining fire, the Godhead, righteousness, mercy, divine light, purification, glory, majesty, or divinity. (Isaiah, Hebrews, Exodus, Revelation, II Chronicles)
- **Green** could suggest New Life, freshness, growing, sowing and reaping, flourishing, prosperity, a new beginning, mercy, vigor, praise, eternal life, health, healing, God's holy seed, or harvest. (Psalms)
- **White** represents purity, righteousness, holiness, triumph, victory, surrender, angels, the Bride, priestly garments, light, or innocence. (Isaiah, Daniel, Matthew, John, Revelation, Ecclesiastics, Zechariah, Psalms)
- **Multi-colors** Leviticus mentions all nations-tribes are represented by multi-colors, apostolic, favor of the Lord, justice.
- **Rainbow** God's covenant promise, the seal of God as shown in Genesis.
- **Tabernacle colors** are mentioned in Exodus 24 times in this order: gold, blue, purple, scarlet, and white.

Be very clear on this: Children are Hebrew thinkers, and hear clearly the simplicity of the Gospel, so the simpler, the better. They are looking for encouragement as much as anything, in a touch from God. And encounter with God is always our goal. Adults are mostly Greek thinkers and therefore want to add lengthy explanations. Nothing I have said here means anything unless the Holy Spirit inspires it. My motto is keep it simple, keep it spiritual!

Children can prophesy to children and it can be more readily received coming from their own peer group, so do not underestimate what God can do through the children in the room. Give kids the freedom to speak out loud what they believe God is telling them. If it is not encouraging then they need to be instructed that God only has good things to say, words of comfort and encouragement. In an adult setting your children need to be taught to speak first to the pastor, and let the pastor release them in a larger setting. We need to create a safe place for children to learn about all their prophetic gifts, but more importantly to learn how to speak out in prophecy.

One boy of about six years old, told me after we had prayed, that he felt lightning bolts go through his body, and then he saw red, blue, green, purple and yellow. Now you could interpret this in many different ways, but keep it simple. God was touching this boy, and showing him the colors that represent God's rainbow, which is God's promise that He knows who you are, and that He will never leave you. Keep it simple, and keep it spiritual.

I simply offer a very brief explanation of what I believe God has shown me over the years. Some people are really into discovering the meanings of the colors and numbers, and there are resources available if you wish to pursue it further. Just remember, Holy Spirit gives the true interpretations of such things.

One of the girls asked me what is a flower or color or symbol for strength.

My reply: The Bible talks a lot about light and the fact that God separated light from darkness. The other thing is from a standpoint of physics, light cannot be separated nor can darkness penetrate it. If you are in the dark all you have to do is turn on a light. Light will always penetrate darkness. So if you want to know about strength it seems obvious that light would be key and point you to yellow. Gold is also significant in the Bible and the yellow hue would thus represent strength because it is light. Notice however that gold was not one of the colors in the rainbow but yellow is. Yellow would also represent life, strength for life or the capacity for life, light and glory.

As far as flowers go, there are many talked about in the Bible, but I would say a rose, a yellow rose in particular. The reason is that the rose represents love and God's desire is that we learn to love the Lord our God with all our heart, soul, mind and strength and to love each other.

So in answer to your question I would say a yellow rose would represent strength.

About that time a nine-year-old walked in and I posed the question to him, he immediately said, "a red rose because Jesus is always strong and red is the color of His blood; He died because He loves us and in Him we are strong." I cannot say that he is wrong. He and I both got something different from Holy Spirit, so both answers are right.

What has God shown you?

The point being just because someone has written an amazing book explaining colors and numbers and symbols do not rely on their interpretation. Get your own from Holy Spirit, and then you will be right for any particular situation.

Chapter 11

Lessons in Art, Dreams & Visions

HE IS DOING THINGS IN POWERFUL WAYS THIS SEASON

God seems to take great pleasure in speaking to children in dreams and visions. Remember, our time with Him is in our quiet time, those times in the first part of the day, right after midnight when we are in a deep sleep. Why? I believe this is the time we can be still and know that He is Lord. We can hear clearly during that time, His still small whisper.

Visions seem to come into view during those times of daydreaming, again a time of stillness. In one of my youth ministry tent revivals, I was sitting on the floor with a very rambunctious, wiggly little four-year-old on my lap. He was sitting with me because he needed to be disciplined so he would not disrupt the other children and distract them from listening to the teacher. He was kind of in a dreamy state, not asleep but not awake, just looking up. All of a sudden, he jumped up and went to the front of the room where one of our teachers was speaking, and he asked to speak into the microphone, and he told everyone to look up at the top of the tent pole. He told everyone to look at the angels who were flying around all of us. Many other children had seen this as well even before he spoke.

Angels are mentioned many times throughout the Bible, and God does speak prophetically through people. Many children have seen angels during ministry times. It is easy for children to see into the spiritual realm. I have seen angels myself. You can do your own research into angels to learn more. I simply add this to prepare you as the teacher, in understanding that this is a big deal to kids, and adults as well! Lord, I pray for angelic encounters.

One time, when I was the last of our group leaving the church, I felt a presence as I was coming out of the prayer room. I saw a big, strong angel, walking beside me; I sensed he was protecting me. He was big and appeared in a kind of trench coat, and he was so tall I could not see his face. I was very much at peace as we walked down the hall together. While the glimpse was quite brief, I sensed his presence all the way down the hall. Another prayer warrior shared she had had a similar experience late one night as she left the prayer room. I am always amazed by God and I pray I never lose that sense of awe that I want to reflect to the children I come in contact with.

An older girl of around fourteen wrote this dream out for me a few years ago. Many children were coming to me with dreams to interpret; I began to have to write them down so I could interpret them later, as there would be too many to get to in one Sunday morning. Her dream went like this:

"I was camping with my friend Torrey and four girls from cheerleading. My brother's boss Hank, another guy, Torrey and I were standing by the river watching Hank. The other guy knocked a dead tree down. There was a bear behind them. I shouted, "Hank, there is a bear," and he and the other guy were trying to scare it away. I turned to Torrey and said, "We need to get out of here." Torrey wanted to stay and watch. I started walking away and she followed but was further behind me. The bear jumped on her. Hank ran up and picked the bear up off Torrey and threw it into the woods. Torrey and I took off towards the camp site. We got there and the girls from cheerleading asked us what had happened. We told them that there were bears and they went to check it out. Torrey and I went inside her tent to gather up any food that would attract the bears. We were looking out the windows of her tent and there were three more bears coming towards us. Then the other cheerleading girls ran up and tried to scare them away. And that's it!"

In my interpretation which I believe was given to me by God; Torrey represents old friends who have shared the same walk with the Lord and Christian principles as the young lady who shared her dream had learned and lived. The cheerleaders represent new friends, who may or may not walk with the Lord, but this was a place for her light to shine. Hank represents authority. The dead tree represents those things on your heart that are hurting; you no longer feel a part of the group. The bear represents all those feelings she could not trust like rejection, being alone, misunderstanding, hurt, and anger. The new friends run to see the bears only because they do not know any better.

The Word, of course, says that you are not to be afraid, that God is with you, caring for your every hurt, your every need.

This girl had been homeschooled and was now attending a public school. So this dream was very meaningful to her.

God has always spoken to us in dreams and visions. He touches our hearts, souls and minds through other people, through our history and it is illogical to think any other way. There are many examples in the Bible of God using dreams, visions, and angels to capture our hearts, our spirits and to speak to us. Think about Joseph in the Old Testament and Joseph and Mary in the New Testament who were visited by angels. Jacob, Samuel and Nebuchadnezzar all had dreams. Daniel witnessed supernatural writing on a wall and Peter had a vision.

There are words of knowledge which are like confirmations of the prophetic for children. Sometimes, kids will smell cookies baking or a beach as they prophesy. The night the Lord healed me of a major illness, I smelled sweet smoky incense that was smelled by others who were present at the time. The point is, just because you have not seen it, does not mean that God is not doing it. Sometimes jewels will appear. One time one of my leaders was covered in gold dust, covered. Many times children witnessed gold dust in our meetings. He is doing things in powerful ways this season and it is sometimes hard to keep up.

Another significant portion of ministry pertaining to youth is with kids in the area of prophetic art, as most kids love to draw and color. The key is to focus that artistic desire through some teachings that are mentioned in the Bible, as an expression of a Biblical principle, to lift up and glorify God. It's not so much what you draw but what you do when you draw. If we do an art seminar or teaching with children, we have continual music worship usually repeating no more than two songs in a session. Be sure to use a worship song. The Lord will unlock their hearts through repetition, and speak clearly to them releasing intercession. Just as dancers release intercession through movements, so these little artists release intercession through creative expression. Prophetic art is just like a prophetic word, in that you must hear God's voice, and draw what He tells you. Yes, sometimes others may laugh at your creation but look what happened to Noah when God told him to build an ark. After all, that is the first record we have of God directing to man to create through art. It is always better to do what God tells you, especially better than self-recognition.

Always ask a child what he was thinking; what was God showing you, what He was telling you as they create their art.

Chapter 12

Fasting-Encountering God's Love

AWAKING THE HEARTS OF CHILDREN

Mike Bickle teaches that fasting is part of the normal Christian life. It is often thought of as an optional discipline. Jesus said, "When you fast," implying that it should occur in the regular course of a disciple's life. He said, *"When you fast, your Father who sees in secret will reward you openly."*

We have taught fasting right along with all the ways God speaks to us through the prophetic. We are taught in scripture to fast and when we explain it, children want to make a love sacrifice for God. Even the very young ones will embrace the concept. Fasting is always about encountering God's love, to encounter more of His heart to change our heart! Having said all of that, I want to be very clear that the Bible never specifically says that children should fast; this is something you have to hear from the Lord clearly for yourself and your ministry team.

We sponsor one of the Signs and Wonders Camps for the International House of Prayer and we always fast the fourteen days before camp. We also set aside special time for fasting as a group when we are in need of a spiritual breakthrough. We encourage the children, our leaders, our intercessors and anyone in the body to join us if God puts it on their heart as a time to fast. Often the children themselves will call for a fast or tell us that God has told them to fast personally for a particular reason.

We ask that they pray to the Lord for what area of their life they are to fast. It could be fasting from specific things such as eating candy, drinking energy drinks, entertainment, etc. **We never encourage children to fast food and we are very clear that it is not something they can or should do.** Equally sacrificial is fasting from a cell phone, texting, video games, TV, music, cartoons, and dating.

In Isaiah 58 we are taught that fasting is to:

Loose the bonds of wickedness—for children **to be set free from bad things**

To undo heavy burdens—children can ask God **to unlock our hearts from problems, bullying, fighting, and divorce**

To help the oppressed go free—**to pray for salvation for a friend, family member, or a nation**

To give bread to the hungry—**to pray for a city, nation, perhaps an upcoming mission trip**

To receive the light of revelation in God's Word—children can learn **to set their heart to know God more**

For emotions and physical health—God's power to **heal someone or for the gift of healing**

For righteousness and break forth—**to encounter more of God**

      Daniel intentionally set his heart to seek the Lord, to humble himself, and pray. We teach that in times of fasting children and adults either spend more time reading their Bibles, praying, or worshiping. So the fast for a child could be, instead of spending thirty minutes watching cartoons, they would spend that thirty minutes reading, praying or worshiping.

      During your time of fasting be sure to have a processing time with the children during and immediately after your fast. Children are so tender to the things of the Spirit. It is amazing the things they share.

      We heard this from a seven-year-old, "I will do my best to be obedient. I will read my Bible. I will find the treasure." An eleven-year-old reported, "Fasting changed my heart and life and made me have a closer relationship with God. I learned how to pray and pray for people better than I knew before. I can't wait until next year." I chuckle to myself; not quite sure why she felt she had to wait until next year?

After a time of fasting, one fourteen-year-old girl told me, "While seeking the Lord one night, God began having me pray for someone who was not seeing well with her eyes." Later we had the opportunity to pray for a lady whose vision was quite cloudy and blurred. The same young girl began interceding quietly in her prayer language before speaking over the lady and blessing her. She came back that evening and came to the girl and asked her to pray again as her sight was improving. The next day this lady gave testimony of healing. This young girl told me she had never openly prayed for anyone and yet God spoke and she obeyed. She has the gift of faith. She has learned to allow the Spirit to control her so fully that this exquisite fruit in her life manifests itself. She is God's instrument. Kids are amazing!

Fasting is always about encountering God's love. The disciples fasted because of their desire to be closer to Jesus. The disciples enjoyed Jesus's presence, feeling His love, and rejoicing in their relationship with Him. Jesus told them that the joy they experienced in His nearness would change to mourning or longing, when He was taken from them by His death. When the joy of His immediate presence had been taken from them, they would be heartsick. To feel his closeness, they could fast!

Fasting awakens our hearts, and our desire for Him. The Holy Spirit reveals the depths of God's love, giving us a hunger for God, based on our desire for Him. When we fast, God increases our desire for Him, and our closeness to Him. Once we taste the nearness of God's presence, we cannot live without more of Him. Fasting tenderizes and expands our hearts to receive from Him. When this occurs, we make thoughtful choices, which lead to different outcomes in the places we go to and the people we meet. When our values are of a Holy influence, it affects who we marry, how we raise children, how we spend our money, and the focus of our ministry.

Important note on fasting: *The level at which a person engages in fasting from food should be determined* *according to age and physical limitations. Those with a physical disability, illness, or eating disorder should not fast, except under the supervision of a physician. Minors are discouraged from fasting food. Minors who desire to fast are encouraged to consider non-food abstentions, such as TV, movies, Internet, video games, and other entertainment. <u>The Bible never says children are to fast food.</u>*

Chapter 13
Caterpillars and Butterflies

FEARFULLY AND WONDERFULLY MADE

-BY TAMMY SEARLE-

I remember one particular spring when I was spending a lot of time in my flower beds and yard, pulling weeds and planting seeds, the Lord had my eyes "spy out" fuzzy caterpillars crawling close to where I was working. My response always was (usually out loud), "Oh, you are going to turn into a beautiful butterfly someday!" I had fun with this every time I saw one and was beginning to think that was a good year for them because I had never seen so many before. I even had one crawling on my jacket sleeve while driving in the car!

As the days played out with my early season garden chores, I began to notice a half dozen or so butterflies fluttering and swooping around me off and on every time I was out there! They were mostly the really big and brilliant yellow Monarch type butterflies! This brought an immediate "thank you" in my heart to God and the truth "that he has started a good work in me and is faithful to complete it". Every time this happens with caterpillars or butterflies, the same thoughts and truths go through my head and heart. I started calling these experiences "Daddy Kisses!" He knows how to delight me in these simple, special ways and it encourages me in my intimate relationship with my heavenly Father.

When Virginia asked me to consider adding a few chapters to her book about mentoring children in the supernatural without a curriculum, it didn't take long for the Holy Spirit to bring back to my memory these and other sweet stories and testimonies. Most of which I believe I wouldn't have to share if I hadn't been gifted with childlike faith and hadn't had the opportunity for the past 14 years to mentor, teach, and love on kids.

Caterpillars turning into beautiful butterflies - a word picture that is a fun way to teach children about their identity in Christ and how valuable and precious they are as a child belonging to God. Perfectly and fearfully made, loved beyond measure just the way they are! If we, both children and adults, can come to understand and really come to know, deep in the innermost parts of our being who we are, how God sees us and feels about us from His perspective, it really is the answer to the abundant life that He died and rose again to give us!

About 13 years ago, I got a phone call from Virginia. She heard that something was going on at this place in Kansas City. She was guided to go to the 24/7 IHOP Prayer Room. She explains to me, through tears, what she was experiencing, "Tammy! There are kids here who are laying hands on people, praying, and prophesying over the adults! I want this for our kids!" I assured her that we would do this with our ministry, and encouraged her to stop crying and come home and we could make it happen.

This marked the beginning of children's church like we had never known before. Did we know what we were doing? Not really. But we got the blessing and go ahead from our leadership and ran with it!

We started encouraging the kids to pray as a group on Sunday mornings; speaking out loud to God of things that they were thankful for, tattle telling on themselves for the things they had said and done that didn't please God, and asking for their wants and needs and those of their family.

We prayed a fresh infilling and baptism of the Holy Spirit over the kids and helped them look up in scripture the truths about their Helper, Comforter, Instructor and Guide.

One of my favorite things we taught and mentored the youth was how to hear God's voice. I had them close their eyes and imagine themselves going into the throne room and crawling up into His lap, then being still and listening! What a blessing when they shared what they heard! Children are naturals at this, and their Heavenly Father is so ready to respond! All it takes is a little encouragement in this way.

In addition to the Sunday morning time, I started meeting with kids who were interested in being part of a children's church praise band. It consisted of my three boys, Virginia's grandkids and all their friends! That was such a rocket ride it deserves an entire chapter all to itself. But first I want to share with you some of what the Lord did as we carried the Kingdom into the public school.

A ruling had come down from the U.S. Supreme Court and we went to our local school board and got permission to hold an after school club in the fall of 2000. The Jelly Beans and Squiggly Things after School Fun Club was born. It was our strategic and intentional way of communicating the gospel to children who do not go to church. We target all school age children but mainly our group consists of kindergarteners through 4th graders. Our Club meets once a week and attracts a lot of kids who do not attend a church. So this unique opportunity has opened the door for a lot of salvation decisions and a special time of sharing Jesus. No particular curriculum or lesson plan has ever been our focus, but rather, encouraging them in developing a relationship with God, Jesus and the Holy Spirit. What we were doing on Sunday mornings spilled over into the club times, too.

I'm a big fan of keeping it real with kids when it comes to teaching children about the things of God, his nature, his character, and personality. Many of these children come from broken and dysfunctional homes. Connecting the heart of a child with the truths and promises of God to their current life experiences can speak volumes to them in the "there's hope" department!

I remember one time a little nine-year-old boy was not picked up when our club time ended. He called his mom and we arranged to have me transport him to meet her up town. During the ten minutes it took to deliver him to her, I asked him how things are going and I'll never forget what he said! He proceeded to tell me that he has been depressed! (I could not imagine a nine-year-old being depressed!) I encouraged him that God loves him very much and the lyrics of a song immediately come into my head. I taught him the lyrics and we sang this song together as we traveled to meet his Mom, "I'm in love with God and God's in love me. This is who I am and this is who I'll be and that settles it, completely!" When we arrived at our destination, before he got out of my car, he looked over at me said, "Ms. Tammy, I'm gonna sing that whenever I start feeling sad." The look on his face was priceless. He had hope. He had a tangible way to deal with life as he knew it and it put God in the center of it! Some months later, I ran into his mom at the market. She shared with me that her son was across the country visiting his dad, and he was homesick. She asked him if he had been saying his prayers and he replied yes. She also went on to share how blessed she was that he learned how to pray and prayed often as a result of being part of the Jelly Beans Club. I could tell that this precious Mother was homesick too, for her little boy and we prayed together right there in the potato chip aisle. She left touched with a little more of God's love in the center of her life too!

One thing that has been proven over and over again to me is that just being available in the life of a child is huge. My husband, Jack and our three boys, Ryan, Riley, and Ryder have all been involved with this after school outreach for 11 years. We have had the awesome blessing of watching our own boys grow in the knowledge and intimacy of God and have relationship with Jesus and the Holy Spirit on a daily basis. It is as simple as just being available and showing up then repeating it the next week, and again and again. If you are reading this book, you obviously have a heart to mentor children in the supernatural. I want to encourage you that you are probably more equipped than you think you are. What you glean on a daily basis in your own personal walk most likely can be dialed down to a first grade level and shared with the children that God has put in your life and sphere of influence. I'll never forget what I heard James Dobson say when I listened to his Bringing up Boys CD series. He said, "That a godly man in the life of a young boy for at least one hour a week can make all the difference in that boy's life." One hour a week! I'm truly grateful for my husband's heart to be the godly father to our boys and to so many other children who affectionately call him the "game guy!" He has faithfully shown up week after week for 11 years (and counting), for games and fun during the club time.

Our sons are 20, 18, and 16 years old now, and fit the definition of godly men. They aren't Jelly Bean Clubbers anymore, but they have been faithful to show up week after week and pour into these smaller saints and make a difference!

In all of our time spent grooming the kid's hearts to carry the presence of, and function in the fruits, and gifts of the Holy Spirit, a few things come to mind that seemed to "amp it up!"

Each child is given a Bible, if they don't have one, and encouraged to bring it to each club time. I have a designated time each week when we break up into small groups and teach them how to look up scripture. They love it, even if they can't read yet! They use colored pencils to highlight the verse and a small sticky note to mark the page. I then teach them how to use that scripture and make it into a prayer and pray it out loud back to God. I encourage them to get into their Bibles when at home, which is easy with highlighted pages and verses, and have a quiet time with God daily. We practice nurturing the quiet place with them.

One day a young boy asked me if he could stay inside and look up scripture instead of go out for the game time! I'll never forget another time, after a boy had received Jesus as his Lord and Savior, I told him his name was in the Bible. I showed him John 1:12 and began reading to him, "But to Johnny who received Him, to Johnny He gave the right to become a child of God, to Johnny who believes in His name." In an instant, he straightened his back, sat up at attention and gasped with surprise and delight! What a blast! A Daddy Kiss and Holy Spirit touch in a "suddenly!"

Using the Word to equip and train up is so effective and powerful! The Holy Spirit does the work! I focus on truths that teach kids who they are, who God is, what He is like, and how He thinks. Search and find scriptures that speak to, and quicken you. Here's a head start: Phil. 4:13, Eph. 2:6, 2Cor. 5:17-21, John 15:16, Phil 3:20, 2 Tim 1:7, Heb. 4:16, 1 John 5:18, Col. 2:10, Col.1:14, John 15:15, Eph. 1:5, Eph. 2:18. Here are some of my favorites on His character and personality. Romans 8:38-39, John 17:23, 1 John 3:1, 1 John 4:16, Psalm 139:1-2, Zephaniah 3:17, Jeremiah 32:41, Jeremiah 33:3, Psalm 37:4, Phil. 2:13, Eph. 3:20, 2 Cor. 1:3-4, Matt. 5:48, Jeremiah 31:3, Psalm 34:18, Romans 8:31, 2 Thess. 2:16-17.

As we continued to consistently show up week after week, before I knew it we were celebrating our 10-year anniversary. I set aside four weeks that year to teach on the book of Revelation. I had recently sat under Mike Bickle's teaching and spent a lot of time in study myself to dial it in to a first grade level. If you teach children, I encourage you to seek Holy Spirit guidance, and dial in! Mike has a teaching library that you can access on the internet at www.ihop.org click on resources and go to Mike Bickle Teaching Library: Book of Revelation: Forerunners Preparing the Bride.

I truly believe as I look into the faces sitting in front of me each week, this is quite possibly the generation with the mandate to hasten the Day of the Lord. This is a generation that will discern the signs of the times and is now being prepared in practical ways for this. I am humbled and blessed that God has given me, my family, and other committed and willing believers, this opportunity of equipping the end time warriors and forerunners. It's exciting! It's fun! It can be understood by all, even a child!

Two weeks into the Revelation study with the kids, I had made it about half way through explaining the seal and trumpet judgments of the Great Tribulation (Rev. 6-9). One particular day I was describing the fifth Trumpet, the release of the demon locusts from the bottomless pit that torment satan's people. The kids were totally engaged and I had their full attention. This one little boy suddenly jumped up out of his seat and waved his Bible back and forth above his head and shouted, "Ms. Tammy, Ms. Tammy can you show me where that's at in my Bible?" My helpers quickly responded to his request and he began to follow along, with great enthusiasm, to God's written description of the end time events! God's heart is for all believers to be prepared as He returns for his Bride and for all to participate in the great end time drama, which we overcome in great victory!

Children are typically not content to be observers. A continual encouragement in the truths of who they are as sons and daughters in God's family and how much they are loved by their Heavenly Father actively engages them. They quickly can understand that God so loves them that he gave them His very own Spirit to live in them! They understand the Holy Spirit gives them comfort and peace and helps them live in communion with Jesus, the One their soul loves.

This time we have set aside weekly, for over 10 years now, has engaged and encouraged children to be "naturally supernatural!" They easily and readily hear God's voice. Prayer is simple for them and they are eager to participate. These weekly prayer times invite the Holy Spirit to hover and minister to the children. They receive. For many of them, this experience is the opportunity for the coming of the Holy Spirit that leads them into a life of prayer. It is so powerful! The children carry these experiences back into their homes. I've had parents share with me how their child is so open and willing to pray at home. They credit it to their time spent in prayer regularly at the Jelly Beans Club. I am grateful and thankful to have the opportunity to minister and work with kids, and for the parents who have trusted and allowed me, my family, and our helpers to pour into their children in this way.

Each week as the club time comes to an end, I routinely remind the kids as they leave, to bring their Bibles back with them next week, along with any prayer requests, too! On this one particular day, as the last child left, I didn't say the usual to her; instead, I just stood in the hallway and watched for a few seconds as she walked away. In the next instant, I heard myself shout after her, with my hands cupped around my mouth in the megaphone type gesture, "Release the Kingdom wherever you go!" She replied, without missing a beat or even turning around, "I will!"

So precious! That "suddenly" exchange of encouragement blessed my socks off! A scene that rewinds and replays often in my Jelly Bean Club highlights archives!

Chapter 14

Fire on the Rock

HANGING OUT WITH CHILDREN OF FIRE

-BY RILEY SEARLE-

Fire on the rock, that statement alone is a testament of God's power. Jesus said that he is the rock where we should build our foundation, and God will release His fire into our lives if we ask Him to. The fire and the anointing were released that night simply because we were obedient to His calling...

I don't know where to start, so I will start at the beginning. We were camping in a location in New Mexico. Our tent meetings at a secluded mountain camp on the reservation are really powerful and of course the children carry God's anointing whenever we go. Why we were out on a rock, singing our hearts out to the Father till four in the morning, I don't know, but I do know that it was God's divine timing, and we were His servants.

As the camp progressed people were getting slain in the spirit and there was a heavy anointing on this night. There were so many of us on that rock, and we have no idea how we all fit other than God must have expanded it to accommodate us all. None of us had any idea what God had in store for us.

At first we were all star gazing, pointing excitedly as we saw a shooting star, but it soon turned into something much more powerful and serious. Junior, a young native warrior, was lying by me and I heard him sobbing quietly. When Silas and I asked him what was wrong he said that his Dad was away. At the time, we just thought that he felt lonely and wanted to be with his Dad but we soon found out that it was just the opposite.

After a while, Junior and Jeffrey, his older brother, wanted to go back up to the tent. Kayley, Kevin, and I took them back up the hill as the others stayed and star gazed. Kayley took them to their Mom as Kevin and I stayed at the tent and got a mid-night snack! As she came walking back to us, she had this sad look on her face. She said that Junior and Jeffrey were scared because their Dad was drunk.

As we walked back to the rock, everyone still laughing and having a good time, I was praying for Junior's Dad. We managed to tell the others, and we all started praying with a passion for the Navajo nation and his family. The prayers continued for about thirty minutes, and when we were done we decided to worship all night; fire on the rock!

We grabbed a guitar, our bibles, sleeping bags and pillows for a little more comfort on the rock. You could feel the presence of God that night as we interceded for the reservation and the family. God was pouring out his spirit on us in such a big way. We took turns playing and singing long into the night as we got visions, prophetic words, and scripture verses for the tribe.

Fire on the rock, as we called it, was an amazing experience! It all happened simply because we were obedient to His calling and we were ready to do His will. I know in my heart that we made a difference that night on the rock, even if we don't see it with our eyes.

"For my thought s are not your thought s, nor are your ways My ways," says the Lord. "For as the heavens are higher than the earth, so are My ways higher than your ways, and My thought s than your thoughts." (Isaiah 55: 8,9)

This is a report from a couple of fifteen year olds, in their own words.

We take a group up on a nearby reservation for a time of camping and ministry each summer. I have included a few more, be blessed:

1. My testimony of the Signs and Wonders was life changing. I know I have been coming to it at least three years but this 2009 Signs and Wonders changed

my life. It helped me to see my calling more clearly. During the services, God just rained down His Spirit. I learned to understand some of my vision. Things sometimes go badly, but it helps me to grow strong. Trials may come but God is always there and never leaving. The Fire in the Night was an experience that I enjoyed. I never knew that I could pray for so much and still have the need for even more. Like I said, it was a life changing experience. Leanna 14

2. We always seem to grow at camp every year. Camp was different this year and very good. We have gone deeper with worship since we left camp and we are trying now to apply the 30 minutes a day time with Jesus that we had committed to before we left. Since we home school we will make it a part of each day before we start our schooling. Thank you so much for all the work, prayers, and fasting put into camp. We will return! Patricia and family

3. The Colorado Signs and Wonders Camp was a wonderful inspiration for me. Not only did God show me the joy of children becoming very close to one another, He showed me the joy of seeing children minister love to each other. That joy was reflected in a beautifully inspired picture of an angel and children dancing for joy. I thank God for the wondrous signs He showed me when there was a 24-hour worship team singing praises to our God. I was awakened every morning with the sound of Angles singing. All Glory to God. Mary

4. I am 14 and God told me to start a 24-hour prayer room at my church so we can be closer to God. I have started making plans for the first prayer meeting on Friday, July 11th, from 7pm-11pm. My Mom took me to all the churches in my area and I invited the pastors and their congregations to the first prayer meeting. We also went to some Christian owned businesses. My Dad is setting up a pod playlist of worship songs I have chosen to play from 7pm to 11pm (I do not have a

worship team yet). I have planned to set up communion, a map of the world, a list of all the churches, and their pastors in my area to pray for, and a table for prayer requests that anyone may want to write down.

Chapter 15

We Do What We Do & That it is All That We Do

MAKE ROOM FOR THE SPIRIT AND LEAVE THE DOOR OPEN

I am sure some of you are thinking "But there is no formula, curriculum, or plan!" All of us who have pioneered in this movement have seriously pondered the whole idea of curriculum and believe that ministry today has to be out of an overflow of what God is doing in our own hearts. Children deserve the very best of what the Lord is doing in our own spirits first. If that makes us out of the box, then we really are out of the box! I have tried to give you some ideas of what I mean, in building your faith. You can do this, but only if you set your heart and allow the Holy Spirit to rise up in you, so that He is the one doing it ALL. I remember at The Call a few years ago, Pastor Lenny LaGuardia and I had around fifty or so kids behind stage waiting for our turn to pray, waiting and waiting. We finally positioned the kids on stage, after a couple of hours of waiting. Lenny was at one end with Pastor Lou Engle and I was at the other, right behind Pastor Mike Bickle. Suddenly, (and God is a God of suddenlys!), Pastor Lou Engle said "Get these kids off the stage because God has just spoken to me and we are to do something else." I love to work with people who easily hear and move when God tells them. Make way for the Spirit; always leave an open door for God.

The first thing you need is a team.

You will need prayer warriors or intercessors, willing to commit to praying for you, your leaders, and your children. They need to be committed enough to spend Sunday mornings in the Children's Equipping Center. Their only job is to pray.

You will also need a worship leader willing to follow you

as the Holy Spirit leads. We train our own kids to play instruments and lead worship following an adult. We offer free lessons on Tuesday afternoon to learn guitar, keyboard, or drums. Our leader has an easy, simple way to teach them and before you know it they are in the rotation as part of the team.

Teachers must be able to commit to every Sunday. Children learn best by building relationships. Relationships require consistency, and relationships require friendships.

Every Sunday may seem too much, but really? This is the most important place of ministry. This is a battle ground for a generation and the attrition rate of teachers is horrible, most only lasting six months, rarely longer. The greatest excuse is that they need to be in church with adults so they can hear the message. The question is then "What are you feeding your children?" Your children should receive just as the adults do. Your friends will become those in the area of ministry you are called to. You should know how to feed yourself on the Word, and move in His presence, submitted to the Spirit continuously.

This is the secret, in the words of my friend, Pastor Lenny LaGuardia, "You show up, you come back and you keep coming back." This is what produces passionate children, and passionate children will produce other passionate children, and it is all about building relationships. When my identical twins were young they did not like going to Sunday school because they always had a different teacher, and they never knew their names! No relationship!

The biggest problem I see in ministry to children on the reservations is that they do not desire to have a relationship with you. Why? Because they know they will never see you again. Children that I have mentored over the years, by going back again and again, are now young adults and we still have a relationship. You have to desire that from the children/youth you are working with. They long to be your friend.

In your Children's Church, after school program or whatever the venue, once our kids understand, and begin to move in the Spirit, they become part of the leadership team.

Children can take a leadership role at an early age and they love to lead. We take them aside one day a week for mentoring in a time of Bible study and prayer for about an hour.

Schedule

We generally use a three-hour schedule as our church service is around 2 ½ to 3 hours. You can tailor it to fit your venue, be it Sunday mornings, a solemn assembly, a conference, a camp, a missions trip, a local after-school club, or a lock-in, all with some variations. Simply adjust the times.

We meet an hour before church, so we can pray together as a leadership team. We pray for the adult service, the children, the worship team, speakers, and volunteers. We anoint the room, the instruments, and the sound system. We invite the Holy Spirit to release his presence in each of us that he might use us as a ministry team. We all share the things the Lord has revealed to us. We pretty much do what we do and that is all we do. We pray, we worship, we teach, we worship, and we pray.

Basically, you will need enough volunteers to gather children in groups of no more than 15. Ideally ten is a good number for the most effective time of ministry.

We never put children in chairs; the smaller the area the easier to mobilize the room. If we have a large room, we face the chairs away from the children and create a barrier. During registration, each group leader has a large number they hold over their heads, that represents a group, and each child is assigned a group at time of registration. Color groups rather than numbers work well with younger children.

As children gather, group leaders are getting acquainted by leading children in hand motions to Apostolic Prayers, which can be tailored so a child understands, or play simple hand clap games. These types of groups are not necessary for the older youth.

Child Protection

It is necessary to adhere to basic Child Protection laws. Be sure each volunteer has a basic FBI background check on file at your church/school/camp. If checking in a large group of children be sure parents sign in, leaving pertinent information on file including a cell phone number. We like to use a two wristband system for parent and child with matching numbers. The Parent or sibling picking up child must have matching number.

You must strictly adhere to no one is left alone with a child. If a child needs a bathroom break he should be accompanied by two leaders.

Basic three-hour schedule:

15-20 minutes of live worship

Your teens will know the fast songs the kids are ready to worship to. Encourage them to move and to dance, to be free before the Lord.

45 minutes of Game Time or Workshop Teaching

These activities help to get the wiggles out, builds relationships, and builds trust.

- **Game Time**
  - Select an adult or mature teen who knows his authority.
  - The Game Leader should prepare ahead of time, anticipating all the options.
  - If indoors again, there are many Relay Races, etc.

- **Workshops**
  - Have two workshops at the same time and give kids a choice.
  - Suggestions would be: Healing, Prophetic Dance, Prophetic Words, Hearing God's Voice, Prophetic Art, Intimacy with God, Beauty of God, or a Guitar Clinic.

If you have a two-hour format, use this time for a fun way to learn a Bible Verse.

30 minutes for bathroom break and snack.

- Everyone should sit in their group after games, and be released by room leader to get snack.
- After everyone has eaten, they can be released again by room leader for group to take bathroom break. Two adults or older teens take the kids; they should not go alone.
- Depending on the facility, one or two teams at a time can use the bathroom.

1 hour and 30 minutes Ministry Time

- The leader controls the room and the worship leader watches room leader and is submissive to his leading during ministry time.
- Begin with the same fast worship song. Repeat the song twice to get everyone's attention. The worship music transitions to very quiet strumming or playing of the worship song selections for the session, no more than two songs.
- The teaching time should be around thirty minutes. Music does not stop, but is quiet and soft during this time. Make sure it is a song that the Holy Spirit will use to engage the hearts of your children.
- Worship should be integrated right into the teaching time. For instance, the room leader will begin encouraging the children and youth that this is their prayer time. Speak prophetically to the group and lead them into a time of ministry, following the guide of the Holy Spirit. Release the group leaders to begin praying for the children. Then, release the children to pray for one another. The room leader is constantly speaking prophetically to all the children as they are praying.
- Through this process we are teaching children the value of prayer and the fruits of the spirit are

released over each of them. We especially like to dwell on the gifts of self-control, gentleness, peace, patience, love, joy, longsuffering.

Parents and release of children

I have a person, usually an intercessor, ask the parents to wait a few minutes until we finish ministry with their child. If they cannot wait, you do have to release the child, however, explain to the parents that it spoils ministry time for the other children. The intercessor's job, remember, is to pray. The person at the door checks the number on the wristband of the child and the parent. Whoever is picking up the child must have a matching wristband.

Chapter 16
Organizing a Sleep Out

HOW TO PLAN A CAMP OUT ONE-O-ONE

It became our philosophy after time, to try to find venues where we could engage more with the children, to not only build relationships but to begin to see these venues as open doors for our training and teaching values, to see children equipped, empowered, and released as leaders among their peers.

We love camping! It takes a little organizing, but once you figure it all out, each year is easier and easier. Ours has been running for over ten years now, so I encourage you to give it a go. This is what has worked for us, and I am sure there are many good books on the subject.

I. POLICIES AND PROCEURES

A. CHILD PROTECTION POLICIES

1. Child Protection is about protecting the local volunteer and the local host.

2. Each person over the age of 18 must be willing to submit to a background check by their specific state. In most states this can be done through the local Sheriff's Department. Most state background checks will tap the National FBI Registry and you do want to make sure this is the case. The cost is nominal. A copy of these background checks should be given to the Director to be filed for 10 years. This needs to be done each year you host a camp.

B. LIABILITY AND HEALTH INSURANCE COVERAGE

1. The amount of coverage required for liability insurance varies from state to state. The liability of your church's policy can be increased for that week if a church is sponsoring the camp. Usually the cost is based on the number of campers attending.

2. If you are renting a camp facility, the owners usually require a certificate of insurance. You can call your insurance company and ask them to send the certificate to the camp.

3. If you are an individual, you will need to check with your attorney about liability.

4. Health insurance is the responsibility of the parent/guardian as indicated on registration. Your church should not assume any insurance liability as it results to health/accident.

5. You can also purchase camper accident and health insurance for campers or staff who do not have insurance coverage for the specific days of camp. There are several insurance companies you can research online. Two that I know of are American Income Life or Brotherhood Mutual Insurance, both easily found online.

C. OSHA - Hazard Communications Standard

1. Modern life would be impossible without chemicals. Plan and inform all volunteers of Hazard Communications Standards. Usually a simple list of products with health related action is sufficient. This might be something your nurse could make available to camp kitchen, or areas where chemicals are stored.

D. PICTURES OR VIDEOS

1. You must have written permission from parent/guardian in order to use pictures taken at camp to be used in promotional material such as Facebook, YouTube, video presentations, newsletters, or other promotion, where other people will see it. We include this on our registration form.

E. CAMPER RELEASE POLICY

1. The person whose name appears on the registration form as parent or guardian is the primary person we would expect to pick up the child at the end of camp or the end of the day if Day Camp.

    a. For day campers, you might consider the Tyvek numbered wrist band so you can cross reference parent and child.

2. If parent or one of the two emergency contacts are not available to pick child up from camp, then a written permission letter signed by parent must be presented. It would be helpful if the parent communicates that need beforehand.

II. PERSONEL

A. INTERCESSORS

1. Our experience teaches the most important aspect of any camp is to have a strong team praying. The intercessory leader needs to be someone very sensitive to the Spirit who is accountable to the Camp Director.

2. The intercessory team needs to begin praying as soon as a camp date is set, and begins to pray

over each application as it comes in.

3. The intercessor leader needs to present prayer action points to your church and keep them updated before and during camp.

4. It is good if you have enough volunteers, parents, kitchen crew, etc., who can assume the responsibility of each team of campers to pray for.

5. The intercessor leader will have to meet with each of these people. We use handouts which are only a guide and we always encourage our intercessors to follow the Holy Spirit's leading first and foremost.

6. We encourage each intercessor to be praying during main session teachings, small group times, and boys and girl's sessions.

7. Team leaders can take the individual needs of their team to intercessors.

8. Ideally a 24-hour prayer room would be going on during the camp time.

B. CAMP DIRECTOR

1. This position needs careful consideration and is the responsibility of the local church that is willing to work with a strong team.

2. The Camp Director needs to possess servant leadership and organizational skills. The objective of the Camp Director is to influence the camp staff and assist in helping them meet the goals of the camp by serving each individual staff member.

3. He/She should be in agreement with the objectives of the Core Value Teaching stated above and pass the required background check.

4. A camp rental facility needs to be secured at least one year in advance if not owned.

5. Plan and present his/her budget to the church for their approval. The Regional Director is available for assistance if needed.

6. Prepare registration forms for mail or email, or download to a church website, and if applicable link to the CEC website.

7. The Camp Director will secure each staff member. Each staff person secured should be in agreement with the objectives of the Core Value Teaching stated above and pass the required background check.

8. The Camp Director is responsible to set up a mandatory training day for all staff approximately one week before camp.

9. It is the responsibility of the Camp Director to make sure all needed supplies are at camp.

10. If you are going to use t-shirts you will need to have a design ready, and facilitate that.

11. The Camp Director will schedule sleeping arrangements for children, counselors, junior counselors, ministry team, and any other personal.

12. Camp Director must oversee registration and check out procedures.

13. He/She must make himself available and sensitive to the needs of the staff and children, counseling if necessary.

14. You will want to have a person assigned to you to

simply be your hands and feet and to meet the needs that you can delegate.

15. It is important to leave the camp clean. Needed supplies for clean-up and maintenance also fall on the Camp Director.

16. Meet after camp with staff and children and debrief, if possible.

C. SENIOR COUNSELOR

1. Must be in agreement with the Core Value teachings and have a passion to see children released as forerunners in who God has created them to be.

2. Needs a sense of humor, patience, high energy level, and willingness to put the child first.

3. Counselor report to the Camp Director.

4. Counselor is to care for the emotional, physical and spiritual needs of his team and campers.

5. Counselor is to be with, and care for, his team/campers at all times, sitting with their team during group times as well as during meals.

6. We believe strongly that it is important to model, teach and train children. Counselors are expected to actively participate during ministry times, worship time, mealtimes and games. Be with the children all the time, all the time be with the children.

7. Supervise bedtime routine for team/campers and keep your team in their cabin or tent at night.

8. Encourage your team to be on time for all camp activities and to follow the camp schedule.

9. Pray for any child or adult reporting accident or illness, and then report accident or illness to the Camp Nurse immediately.

10. Maintain discipline within your team and report difficult discipline cases to the Camp Director.

D. JUNIOR COUNSELOR

1. Must be in agreement with the Core Value teachings and have a passion to see children released as forerunners in who God has created them to be.

2. Minimum age is 14 and evidence a love for children at the discretion of the Camp Director.

3. To be responsible to the senior counselor and then to the Camp Director.

4. To help in the general care of your assigned team/campers under the leadership of the senior counselor.

5. We strongly believe it is important to model, teach and train children. Junior counselors are expected to actively participate during ministry times, worship time, mealtimes and games. Be with the children all the time, all the time be with the children.

6. Sit with your team of campers at all assigned meetings.

7. Enforce camp routines, schedules, and regulations by modeling, be an example.

8. Provide total cabin leadership in the absence of the senior counselor and be an example at all times.

E. GAMES ACTIVITY DIRECTOR

1. Must be in agreement with the Core Value teachings and have a passion to see children released as forerunners in who God has created them to be.

2. To plan and organize the camp games under the direction of the Camp Director.

3. To prepare the activity, have available all needed equipment and be prepared to teach or facilitate the activity.

4. Love and encourage the children and possess the ability to work with them.

5. Set-up and put away all equipment.

F. CAMP NURSE

1. Must be in agreement with the Core Value teachings and have a passion to see children released as forerunners in who God has created them to be.

2. Check with your state regulations. Most states only require someone who is licensed in first aid and CPR.

3. All emergency contact information needs to be immediately available to the camp nurse which would include the nearest doctor, hospital, and information for the children.

4. Camp Nurse is to screen all the campers as they register and review the campers' and counselors' confidential medical history. The church you are a part of should keep these on file during camp and place in a permanent fil e following camp.

5. Notify counselor of any special needs or conditions.

6. Notify kitchen of any special diets.

7. Set up a well-marked area for the administration of first aid and medicines. Organize a careful record of all services performed regarding accidents and treatment. Include name, cabin or team, date, time, why they came, and treatment given. Report all accidents to the Camp Director.

8. Have basic aid supplies available where children are.

III. ROAD BLOCKS TO COMMUNICATIONS

A. Camp Director is here to serve the church staff, and camp leadership. It is important to stay in communication by asking questions.

B. One month before camp, an all camp staff meeting is important to make sure everyone is on the same page and all issues clearly addressed.

C. One week before camp, it is again necessary for an all staff meeting.

IV. TIPS FOR AGE GROUP

A. Children seem to do best with other children their age overall. It is better if you can assign children with the group they came with; hopefully, with a leader from their home church.

1. Ideally, you will have one adult and one junior counselor for each eight to ten children, but we have had as many as fifteen to a cabin with one adult and two junior counselors who are well trained.

2. If the dynamics are not there for some children to be with their group, perhaps they came alone, always try to find out if they have a friend at Signs and Wonders Camp, and then place them accordingly.

3. Some children will come not knowing anyone and it is vitally important that the counselor is aware to give that child special attention. It is recommended that the child is placed in a cabin with children the same age.

4. Some camps take children as young as seven as long as they bring a parent. The family usually stays at a hotel and joins camp for the day.

5. Younger children seem to do better if games are selected with ages in mind.

V. FINANCE PROCEDURES/BUDGET FORM

A. Finance Procedures

1. Generally, once the price of the camp is set, the application will require a $25 deposit and the balance due one week before camp.

2. All forms must be filled out completely before child is accepted as a camper. This is extremely important and saves a lot of last minute work. Assign one person to collect applications and process them. Confirmation can be sent via email.

3. Generally, a date is set one month out from the day of camp for all applications to be in. Those not in by this date are subject to a late registration fee, usually $50.

4. It will be up to the individual church, but you should plan on whether or not to offer some scholarships

for some families.

    5. A typical budget form works well.

  B. Honorariums, Travel and Lodging

    1. All honorariums are to be covered in the budget and based on registration fees as discussed initial consultation.

    2. Travel arrangements should be discussed with the Regional Director. Tickets are secured by the host co-coordinator or church.

    3. Arrange for someone to pick team up and return them to the airport.

    4. Lodging at a motel is ideal.

VI. FOOD

  A. Children like simple food. If you are preparing for a group simple cost effective menus are available on line. We can feed kids for around $6 to $8 per day.

  B. You will want to have a full team, if you are preparing food for the campers.

  C. Parents who come for camp and wish to help can be used here.

  D. I like to use each team of campers at least once in the kitchen to help with clean-up. This is a good teaching tool for them as well.

  E. If you are renting a facility, the food is usually included.

VII. LOGISTICS

    1. Look at your budget to see if the vision will come to pass.

2. What needs are to be met in order to facilitate the camp, such as, fund raising, donations, scholarships, etc.

3. Secure your facility.

4. Appoint Intercessor and begin interceding as you continue to express needs, praises etc.

5. Appoint Camp Director Position. Camp Director begins immediately to fulfill needs of his position.

6. Develop forms and publish on your webpage, decide on advertising.

7. Keep in contact with the local host church leadership with progress, questions, or any help needed.

8. Schedule airline tickets and someone to come for training one month before camp.

Chapter 17

How to Chase After God's Heart

HOW TO BE A MAN/WOMAN AFTER GOD'S HEART

"Elijah saw the thunder in the mountains in 1 Kings 19; the thunder, and the storm, and the fire, and the rain, and the sweet whisper. I love the thunder and the lighting and the earthquake, but I tell you, I love God's sweet whisper: "I especially like you." The Lord's capacity is so great that He especially likes every one of us who will say yes back to Him. It is then that you receive His special love. That's so wonderful. It makes everything so different".

I am including this sermon titled "How to be a Man/Woman after God's Heart" written by Pastor Mike Bickle simply because it is so true as it relates to you and to me but more importantly this is a message for this generation. This should be our heart in order to impart to a generation.

"Turn to 1 Samuel 13. I want to introduce to you a man whom the majority of you already know. It's King David, the great warrior-king of Israel. David is about fourteen or fifteen here. He might be younger; no one knows for sure. The Spirit of the Lord comes upon a prophet named Samuel, the anointed prophet Samuel. The Lord whispers in Samuel's ear and says, *"I'm replacing the rebellious king, Saul."* He says, "I've found a young man who has a heart after Me. He doesn't even know that I've found Him" (1 Sam. 13:14, paraphrased).

There are many mysterious points to this verse. One of the mysteries of this verse is that David is fifteen years old on the backside of some hill in Bethlehem. I mean, Bethlehem has 300 people; it's Hooterville minus one. I mean it's really bad; it's really little. It's a poor, out-of-the way, a nowhere place. He's the youngest of eight brothers. He's always left out. Many times in his family he's picked on, made fun of. It's a real deal. He's the youngest. It's a very poor family, in a tiny, 300-person town. He does the most boring job: he tends sheep all day by himself.

He made a little guitar; it probably wasn't much, considering his poor family. He began to look up at the stars at night and say, "O, I love You. I don't know You, but I love You. I want to know You. What are You like? Who are You? What's going on?" Something was moving in this young guitar player's heart at age fourteen or fifteen, in this very poor, out-of-the-way, boring little town with a very boring job in this poor family.

God whispers to the prophet Samuel, "That kid over there, that guitar player who doesn't know that I've heard his voice; I like him! He has a heart for Me. I've taken note of that kid. I want you to announce who he is to the rebellious king Saul. I want you to tell him one day when you meet him what I think about him."

David becomes the picture of the end-time church. The Church that the Lord is raising up before the Lord returns is a church after God's own heart, like David. Look at what God tells Samuel: *"The Lord has sought for Himself a man after His own heart"* (1 Sam. 13:14, NKJV).

He has sought for Himself a man after His own heart. What does it mean to be a person after God's own heart? The life of David is a very, very important place of study in the Word of God. David is the great worshiping warrior.

I love to talk about the gladness of God's heart; it's one of my favorite messages, the glad heart of God, because today many, many people believe God is mostly mad or mostly sad when He relates to them. I have good news for you: He's mostly glad when He looks at you. It changes everything because you run to Him instead of from Him. When mom or dads are angry you want to stay away, in your room or anywhere else. If God's mostly mad and mostly sad, you turn around and run from Him. I so loved to be loved. I'm just like you; I love to be loved, it's such a wonderful way to live. Really!

In the Bible when David did things he knew he shouldn't he would walk boldly forward and say to God, "Father, Abba, here I am. I've sinned, I can't believe I did that, I love You, God! It's my weakness. God sometimes I think, say and do things I know are wrong. God, I know that in Your infinite mercy You want me. I want You!" He had this confidence as a lover of God that's found nowhere else in the Old Testament. David's confidence as a lover in his weakness is absolutely amazing.

He wasn't just confident that God loved him; he knew that God enjoyed him. We hear the phrase, "God loves me," all the time, but now begin saying "God enjoys me." That pushes it a little. God enjoys me even in my weakness when I think, say and do things I know are wrong. It's not enough to know that God enjoys me and to have confidence that He actually likes me while I'm growing up. It's more than that. When my love for Jesus is weak, it's still real. We have this idea that our love isn't real until we grow up. One of these days when I'm sixty, and my love is mature, then it's real. Most adults I know think that love isn't real until love is mature. I do not agree. I believe that as soon as you begin to love the Lord with all your heart, soul, and mind, God will use you. Let me tell you, your weak love is authentic, it's real, and it's genuine even when it's weak. It's more than, "I need to have confidence that God loves me, God enjoys me, God calls me His friend."

You have to have a second thing: confidence that God believes I love Him even when I'm young. When I stand before God in my weakness, I stand loved, but I stand not just as one who just receives love. I am loved, but He sees me as an authentic lover even when I'm just a kid. He says, "Your love is real. I know that you love Me. You're not just pretending under grace; you're a genuine lover who is still young." When I feel loved and I know that I'm a lover in return, my heart is alive! I say, "I love this! I love the Holy Spirit and the grace of God! I can do anything if that's the relationship!" That's the way that David lived before God.

David was a man after God's own heart. There are two different definitions I like to use for a person after God's own heart. This is really important for you, because the Church worldwide is a people after God's own heart like David.

1. David was a man after God's own heart because he obeyed the commands of God's heart. There was a yes in his spirit to the Word of God. There was a commitment to obedience. He obeyed the commands of God's heart.

2. David studied the emotions of God's heart. He was a man going after what was burning in God's heart. David would tell God, "I want to know what You feel! I want to know what You're thinking! I want to know what You're feeling! I want to know Your heart!" David became a student of the affections of God.

God is raising up an army of radically dedicated young people who are students of the affections of God. I just want to pause a second; I want you to all close your eyes for just one moment. In your own soul, I want you to say something to the Lord: not my words, but yours.

Quietly you'll say, "I want to be a student of Your affections and Your emotions. I never thought about that, but I want to be a student. Lord, I want to be like David; I want to do this. I don't know how to do it, but I want to do it. If someone will tell me how to do it, I'll do it. I want to know Your heart."

David was certainly one of the most unique men in the Old Testament. There was no man in the Old Testament who had understanding of God's emotions like King David, no one. He stood in a class of his own. I mean, Moses has all of these really powerful encounters with the Lord. David comes along about 500 or 600 years after Moses. David gets so much more understanding of God's heart than Moses had. He brings the kingdom of God to an entirely different level. No one after David, none of the great prophets, no one received greater understanding of God's heart in the Old Testament than King David, *"the man after God's own heart."*

Here's what God wants us to do. God wants us to be a

people after His own heart. He wants us to obey the commands. That was the secret of David's life. David wanted to know more than the what of God. He wanted to know God's power. He wanted to know the why of God. He didn't just want to know that God had the power and the wisdom to create the heavens and the earth. He loved the what of God's power. God created everything and He saved us. David leads history in works and miracles.

What did God do? What God does is a powerful subject. I want to know something more than what He does; I want to know why He does it. "What are You feeling when You create the heavens and the earth? When You used Your power to make stars and galaxies and the earth for the human race, what were You feeling? I want to know that, because it matters to my life to know why You did this thing called making me. Did You make me to display Your power in making humans? Or did You make me and other humans because You longed with desire for humans?" Stop and be still before the Lord and ask Him to reveal this to you.

The Lord's answer is this: "I desired for humans. I wanted them; I wanted them. I want you; in your weakness, even when you think, say, and do things you know are wrong. I want you. When others don't want you, I want you." When you know what God's heart looks like emotionally and you know what you look like spiritually to God, then, you will want to chase after God. You'll never, ever get anyone to change their actions long term until they change the way they view themselves before God.

Let's look at Psalm 16

1. *Keep me safe. O God. I've run for dear life to you.*
2. *I say to God, "Be my Lord!" nothing makes sense*
3. *And these God-chosen lives all around-what splendid friends they make!*
4. *Don't just go shopping for a god. Gods are not for sale. I swear I'll never treat god-names like brand names.*
5. *My choice is you, God first and only. And now I find I am your choice!*
6. *You set me up with a house and yard. And then you made me your heir!*

7. The wise counsel God gives when I'm awake is confirmed by my sleeping heart.
8. Day and night I'll stick with God. I've got a good thing going and I'm, not letting go.
9. I'm happy from the inside out. And from the outside in, I'm firmly formed.
10. You canceled my ticket to hell, that's not my destination!
11. Now you've got my feet on the life path, all radiant from the shining of your face. Ever since you took my hand, I'm on my way.

David says, *"In Your presence is fullness of joy"* (Ps. 16:11b). This was one of the secrets of David's life, that he understood God's emotions. He said, *"You're a God of gladness; You're overflowing with gladness."* David says, *"Let me tell you about the God for whom I'm lovesick. He's a God of overflowing gladness."* THE CLOSER WE GET TO THE THRONE OR THE MORE YOU PRESS IN TO GOD, THE HAPPIER YOU ARE.

Now let's look at the door to heaven through Revelation 4

¹Then I looked, and, oh! —a door open into Heaven. The trumpet-voice, the first voice in my vision, called out, " Ascend and enter. I'll show you what happens next."

²⁻⁶I was caught up at once in deep worship and, oh! —a Throne set in Heaven with One Seated on the Throne, suffused in gem hues of amber and flame with a nimbus of emerald. Twenty-four thrones circled the Throne, with Twenty-four Elders seated, white-robed, gold-crowned. Lightning flash and thunder crash pulsed from the Throne. Seven fire-blazing torches fronted the Throne (these are the Sevenfold Spirit of God). Before the Throne it was like a clear crystal sea.

⁶⁻⁸Prowling around the Throne were Four Animals, all eyes. Eyes to look ahead, eyes to look behind. The first Animal like a lion, the second like an ox, the third with a human face, the fourth like an eagle in flight. The Four Animals were winged, each with six wings. They were all eyes, seeing around and within. And they chanted night and day, never taking a break:

> *Holy, holy, holy*
> *Is God our Master, Sovereign-Strong,*
> *The was, The Is, The Coming*

> *9-11Every time the Animals gave glory and honor and thanks to the One Seated on the Throne—the age-after-age Living One—the Twenty-four Elders would fall prostrate before the One Seated on the Throne. They worshiped the age-after-age Living One. They threw their crowns at the foot of the Throne, chanting,*

> *Worthy, O Master! Yes, Our God!*
> *Take the glory! The honor! The power!*
> *You created it all;*
> *It was created because You wanted it.*

Think about the throne of God in Revelation 4; the closer they get to the throne, the happier they are. If you were to be transported by the Holy Spirit to the throne of God right now, you would be shocked by the feeling of happiness that you would have. You would have overwhelming terror of God's majesty and an overflowing happiness. You would be saying, "More, I can't handle any more! Too much! Never enough! It's too much, I can't handle it! I want more! Oh, get me out of here! It feels so good! Oh, it's so horrifying!" because it is so intense. Let's forget all of that for now, but if you got up there, you would say, "This is intense!"

Someone says, "What are you feeling?" "I love it up here! I just feel good." Here are the elders; they're falling down. Oh my goodness, he's smiling! Are you happy?"

He gets up and says, "The closer we get, the happier we are; it's incredible!" In His presence, around His throne, is the fullness of joy! The angels in His presence are full of joy. Jesus at the right hand says, "Oh Father, I love You."

The Father says, "Oh, Jesus, I love this! I love My kingdom, I love You, I love the angels, I love My people! This is awesome!"

God is angry at rebellion or the things we think, say and

do that are not allowing us to have close friendship with him. Hebrews 1:9 in essence says this: "Jesus was the happiest Man who ever walked on planet earth" (Heb. 1:9, paraphrased). That's what it says: "Jesus had more of His Father's gladness than any man who ever walked on planet earth." Picture Jesus: this thirty-year-old Man comes into town. He has the brightness of His Father's countenance. He understands human weakness; He likes us; He loves us. This is the God that David worshiped.

Jesus walks into town and has more gladness. He's anointed. It's not just that He has gladness; He has His Father's gladness. It's not like His Father is saying, "There He goes again, my son." The Father says, "That looks just like Me; that's how I feel." Jesus was anointed with His Father's gladness. You are His brother and you too are anointed, it says in Genesis you were born blessed.

"God, there are one billion galaxies in Your power. I love all of that, but the part that I really like—tell me that one part again, that You really, really like me." That's my favorite part of the whole gospel: "I really like you." it really is. We never outgrow the thrill of the wonder of being loved. It's so wonderful to feel loved. It's an absolutely wonderful way to live. The God of love made us to long to be loved. It's wonderful to feel love. I didn't say it's wonderful to be loved, because God loves His people, but most of them are so disconnected from that, that even though He loves them, they can't feel it. I'll add a word; it's wonderful to feel it. You'll never outgrow it. I'll never outgrow it. You'll never outgrow it".

I, Virginia, share this only to encourage you as the teacher to feed yourself daily on God's Word.

I have to share the first time I met Pastor Alan Hood just so you can see the over flow of his heart. It was at this first Children's Pastors Conference at IHOP back in about 2001. The group was quite small and the straight chairs were not very comfortable so I sat on the floor at the front of the room right in front of the speaker Alan Hood. He would walk toward me and I would say, "Oh, Lord let him come closer, I want to get what he has. As he got closer I would start crying and I can't contain the power of your anointing". Then I would say, "Oh, Lord have him walk away, I cannot bear any more. As soon as he would start walking away I would be sad and cry out for more." This is what I so desire for our children, it has always been the desire of our Father in Heaven. You can only teach out of an over flow of what God is doing in and through you just as God did with David.

This teaching is by Pastor Mike Bickle and he has so many teachings you can glean from on the IHOP website, which are free. International House of Prayer at www.ihop.org go to Mike's Teaching Library.

Chapter 18

Strategic and Intentional Effort

YOU CAN DO THIS!

My son and daughter in law are missionaries with Youth with a Mission and were in a country considered closed to the gospel for many years. Their objective was to gather as many as they could and mentor them into the Kingdom. It was a strategic and intentional effort to bring the gospel into a place and seeing people worship God. This was their part in fulfilling the great commission which we are all instructed in the gospels of Matthew, Mark, Luke, John and Acts by the word "GO". I do not think Jesus meant for some of us to go, after all, if you study the scripture you see there were many more there than just the twelve disciples. I think what he was saying was something like, "You guys have seen me, you know me, you love me and now you understand what has happened. Now go, run, take this truth and tell everyone you meet. You can do this! You can do this! I will be with you every step of the way. Just ask me and I will be there using you just as the Father used me, speaking through you, using my power to touch everyone you ask me for. Now go, tell everyone you meet about me, you can do this!"

I told my pastor, my heart was to only do missions, yet I felt led to take on the responsibility of Children's Pastor at my church, with a mindset of missions. We hung a large world map in our prayer room and the children would pray for the missionaries our church supported by laying hands on the map or on their picture. We prayed for their work, protection, financial needs, and so forth, but the thing that stuck out to us was that they really pressed in to the children on the mission field. They were struck with passion for them as families serving God. Three of our missionaries had children in foreign lands and many of us were coming and going with our own children or children from the church. These were their friends, and missions were coming alive to them. Children praying for children! Children with a heart for missions.

It is amazing to me to know that when you talk to missionaries who have been on the field, it seems no matter how remote the area, you can always find a Coke there! Revelation 7:9, *"I looked again. I saw a huge crowd, too huge to count. Everyone was there—all nations and tribes, all races and languages. And they were standing, dressed in white robes and waving palm branches, standing before the Throne and the Lamb...."* If indeed it is our goal to reach all unreached people groups, I wonder how it is that Coke can be there but not the Gospel?

An unreached people group is defined by the Joshua Project as a people group where there is no local native or national led church. Joshua Project also considers about 8,890 people groups unreached. (About 2.83 billion people) Did you know 86% of the world's Muslims, Hindus, and Buddhist do not even know a Christian? Did you know that 87% of cross cultural foreign missions is among nominal Christians? Is it that the easy places have been reached? Between 1988 and 2008, the number of U.S missionaries has dropped about 45%; most missionaries retired and few took their place. Did we miss a generation in the church with a passion to see Jesus made famous in all the earth?

Did you know for every 1,000,000 Muslims in the world there are approximately 3 missionaries? I have heard there is around 5,000 workers per million in our North American population yet some unreached countries have few or no workers. Statistically, only one out of ten cross cultural missionaries will serve the unreached people groups in the world. Does that mean that God loves the people in the US and Canada, more than say Asia, Central Asia, Northern Africa or Indonesia where there is relatively little to no work? In the US and Canada, we have such availability to the gospel through other Christians, many different churches, we have bibles, books, DVD's, Christian TV, and many missionaries. I was at a book fair in a country where little work is done, and there was not one book relating to the truth of who God is. Does that mean that God loves the people in the US and Canada more than Iraq, Iran, Turkey or Saudi Arabia where there is relatively little to no work? If Coke has made it all around the world, why hasn't the gospel?

Living in the Southwest Colorado it was easy for us to give our children a cross cultural experience because we have five reservations in our backyard. Over the years I had developed relationships with many leaders in the area through another ministry. I began taking small groups of children to just hang out and develop friendships. We began to be invited to tent meetings and camps on the reservation, and before you know it, we started our own camp in the area every summer. My strategic and intentional effort was twofold.

1. That our children would experience the difference between two cultures and their hearts would be broken. That they would honor Jesus by developing a passion to heal the sick, reach the lost, prophesy, raise the dead, and see nations transformed.

2. Secondly, my strategic and intentional action involved making disciples of the children we were working with who would desire to do great things for God.

3. That we would go, that we would go back again, and that we would keep going back as our children grew.

For me, I guess the greatest thrill of all is seeing a child who really knows God and understands they are children of God. If we will train our children to know that they are loved by God, we will begin to see young men and women who will desire to do great things for God. We have seen so many young people doing Youth with A Mission, Discipleship Training Schools, Internships at International House of Prayer or Bethel, serving in missions all over the world now, some in the marketplace, operating in the fullness and knowledge of the love of God. We see signs, wonders and miracles as God empowers so many young ones to live out the realities of who they were created for and their purpose in a generation, who have been strategically placed for this hour in history. I believe the secret lies in teaching them to pray, how to hear God's voice, and to lay down their rights in order to honor God by giving their lives in order to make Jesus the Famous One in all the earth. This is what we were created for, "To love the Lord our God with all our heart, soul, mind and strength."

For further reading:

Is That Really You, God? by Loren Cunningham, YWAM.org Making Jesus Lord, by Loren Cunningham, YWAM.org Spiritual Warfare, by Dean Sherman, YWAM.org

Good Morning Holy Spirit, by Benny Hinn

Prayer Leaders Manual, Lenny La Guardia, IHOPKC.org

Praise Leaders Manual, Lenny La Guardia, IHOPKC.org

Here I Am The One You Love, Stephanie Schureman, IHOPKC.org

Releasing Children In Praise & Power (CD Set) Lenny La Guardia & Wes Hall, IHOPKC.org

Biblical Foundations Child: Moses Vol 1, Lenny La Guardia, IHOPKC.org

Loving Our Kids On Purpose, Danny Silk, IHOPKC.org

Raising Spiritual Children, Greg and Patty Mapes, IHOPKC.org

Passion For Jesus, Mike Bickle, IHOPKC.org

Song of Songs (Notes), Mike Bickle, IHOPKC.org

The Bride, Rhonda Calhoun, IHOPKC.org

Adventures with the King, by Patricia King, XP Media

When Heaven Invades Earth by Bill Johnson

The Message Bible, Eugene Peterson

Boy's Passage, Man's Journey, Brian Molitor

Girl's Passage, Father's Duty, Brian Molitor